Instant Pot Diabetes Cookbook for Beginners

120 Quick and Easy Instant Pot Recipes for Type 2 Diabetes

| Diabetic Diet Cookbook for The New Diagnosed

Blair Drake

Chapter 1 The Instant Pot for Diabetes

Why Instant Pot Cooking?

If you've never tried cooking with an Instant Pot before, you might find yourself wondering whether or not it's really worth it. However, most people who use an Instant Pot regularly are more than happy with the results and enjoy the ease with which they can prepare a variety of foods.

When you cook with an Instant Pot, you can save time and make your favorite meals more easily than ever before. Instant Pots also don't take up much room, so you don't have to worry about a large appliance on your countertops either. There are tons of reasons to try Instant Pot cooking, and if you're getting started with a diabetic diet, you may find even more benefits than you expect!

Buttons and Features

Below, you'll find information on some of the many buttons and features you can enjoy with your Instant Pot. Although all models are slightly different, they share many similarities as well.

- Instant Pot models all have buttons that allow you to choose the type of food you're cooking or the type of cooking you want to perform. These may vary slightly depending on the model of Instant Pot you have, but they usually include:
  - Manual
  - Sauté
  - Slow Cook
  - Poultry

- Bean/Chili
- Meat/Stew
- Soup
- Rice
- Multigrain
- Porridge
- Steam
- Yogurt
- Instant Pots also have buttons that let you control the pressure level and amount of time you'll need to cook the food in question.
- Some Instant Pots have digital displays and others do not, but they all have user-friendly button controls on the front of the pot that make them easy to understand.
- Instant Pots also come with a sealing lid that has a steam release button. The auto-sealing lid ensures the perfect, safe seal for every pressure-cooking task, and the steam release vents steam safely away from any users.
- Your Instant Pot will also come with a stainless-steel cooking pot that is easy to clean and take care of.

Benefits of Instant Pot Recipes for Diabetes

The Instant Pot is convenient for any home chef, but for a diabetic diet, it has even more uses.

- Easy, quick meal prep. The Instant Pot makes it easy for you to create delicious meals without much time. Since the cooking pot is insulated, it heats up fast, and it can boil and cook more quickly than other cooking appliances.

- Lots of options. With so many different buttons and modes to choose from, your Instant Pot can help you find unique and tasty ways to enjoy the foods that are healthy for your diabetic diet. You'll be able to prepare tons of meals all with just one pot.
- Nutrient retention. Since the food in a pressure cooker like the Instant Pot cooks fast, it retains a lot more of its nutrients and vitamins than food prepared in other methods. This is great for diabetic dieting, since it means you'll be able to get all the healthy ingredients you need to safely and effectively manage your diabetes through the food you eat.
- Plenty of flavor. Best of all, when you cook with an Instant Pot, this cooking method also retains a lot of flavors. Your food doesn't have to be boring or dull, and you don't have to be stuck with the same few bland meals just because you're eating a diabetes-friendly diet. Your Instant Pot can help your food become more flavorful and vibrant than ever before!

Maintenance

Proper maintenance for your Instant Pot is important in ensuring it remains functional and healthy for you to cook with. However, maintenance is quick and easy when you take care of your Instant Pot.

The lid, steaming rack, sealing ring, and cooking pot portion of the Instant Pot are all dishwasher safe. You can also wash them by hand with hot, soapy water if you prefer (or if you don't have a dishwasher).

Before cleaning any parts of your Instant Pot, make sure to unplug it and let it cool fully for your safety. After cleaning, be sure everything is completely dry before replacing it.

Do not use scrubbing pads on the inner cooking pot. Soak it in water or white vinegar if you're having trouble removing some stains from the pot.

Remove the silicone cap from the float valve before rinsing it out. Replace the float valve before operating the Instant Pot again.

Always make sure your sealing ring is properly reinstalled after cleaning to prevent any accidents with the Instant Pot. Replace it every year or sooner if it becomes cracked or damaged.

Wipe down the outside base of the Instant Pot with a damp cloth. Never submerge the base in water and never use a soaking cloth on it.

Instant Pot Tips and Warnings

Keep these important warnings and tips in mind to ensure the safe operation of your Instant Pot.

- Always thoroughly read the instruction manual before you start using the Instant Pot.
- Do not fill the Instant Pot all the way to the max fill line, especially if you're using it to cook pasta, oats, or rice.
- Take care to never open the Instant Pot in your face or in the direction of anyone else either.
- Never cook with less than one cup of liquid in the Instant Pot.
- Never leave home with your Instant Pot running. You don't have to stand there and watch it the whole time it cooks, but you should be available in case anything goes wrong.
- Like any type of pressure cooker, the Instant Pot can potentially explode when misused. Be sure you understand all of its safety features to prevent this from happening.
- If you use the quick release function on your Instant Pot, be sure to wear a protective glove so you can avoid steam burns on your hands.

Chapter 2 Diabetes 101

In this chapter, we'll take a brief look at diabetes and help you better understand your diagnosis. Be sure to check out the sections on diabetic dieting and which foods to eat and avoid later on in this chapter as well.

What Does It Mean to Be Diagnosed with Diabetes?

If you've been diagnosed with diabetes, chances are good you already have some basic understanding of what this disease means. But many adults with a diabetes diagnosis are unclear about the meaning or find themselves with more questions than answers moving forward. If this sounds like you, then don't worry—you're not alone.

Diabetes is a disease that is related to the content of sugar in your blood, which is also called blood glucose. Although blood glucose is an important part of the energy your body receives from food and uses every day, it's very easy for blood glucose levels to run too high. This happens when your body doesn't produce enough insulin to help convert the sugar in food to energy for your body.

In other words, when your body is unable to use glucose for energy, it stays in your blood and causes your blood sugar to rise. This can become very dangerous if left unchecked, and permanent high levels of blood glucose in your body can cause you to become diabetic.

There are two main types of diabetes. Type 1 diabetes occurs from birth or from a very young age, while type 2 diabetes can occur at any point and is more common in older adults. Both types require multiple methods of treatment for the individual to stay alive and well.

Treatments for Diabetes

These are just some of the treatments you may incorporate as you work toward managing your diabetes.

- **Medical Treatment**
  - Anyone with type 1 or type 2 diabetes should monitor their blood sugar levels and work with a trusted doctor to figure out the right medical treatment plan. You will also need to have your A1C levels checked via lab work frequently.
  - In addition to blood sugar checks, you may need to go on insulin injections if your diabetes is severe. Type 1 diabetics will probably need to stay on insulin from initial diagnosis and throughout the rest of their lives. Type 2 diabetics may be able to avoid insulin through other treatment options.

- **Diet Treatment**
  - There are many methods of managing your diet, and watching what you eat can play a major role in helping you treat and take care of your diabetes. When you stick to a carefully planned diet that is high in nutritional value, you can improve your diabetes symptoms and feel better at the same time.
  - It's important to eat plenty of vegetables and some fruits on a diabetes diet. You should also focus on whole grains and leaner proteins, while avoiding proteins that are known for a higher fat count. Carbohydrates and sugars should be cut down significantly, but still eaten in moderation, while high-fiber foods with lots of

nutritional value should make up the bulk of your diet.

o Understanding what to eat when you're diabetic can be extremely challenging, especially at first. This is why it's a good idea to formulate the perfect meal plan from day one by putting together an arsenal of go-to recipes. This way, you'll never find yourself without the right food for any given day or meal, and you can always have a recipe ready for just about any situation that comes your way.

- **Physical Activity**

o Along with monitoring your diet, you should also add exercise and physical activity to your diabetes treatment plan. When you exercise, your body utilizes the sugar from food by turning it into energy to power your activity. By doing this regularly, you can cut down on the amount of blood glucose in your body and reduce the effects of your diabetes.

o Your doctor can help you figure out the best exercise plan based on your current activity levels and your other health concerns. Most individuals with diabetes should try to exercise at least 15 minutes per day, but some may need more activity than this.

Diabetes Nutrients

Pay attention to these nutrients, as they are all some of the most important in a diabetic diet.

- **Macros**

o **Carbohydrates:** Carbs can give you energy. They help your body maintain its metabolism and improve brain functionality at the same time. There are two different types of carbs, however, and it's important to focus on the "healthy carbs" when you're eating a diabetic diet.

- Fibrous carbs are slow to digest and are much healthier for you than the alternative. On a diabetic diet, you should focus as much as possible on fibrous carbs to cut down on the feeling of hunger throughout the day and improve your physical health and energy.
- Starchy carbs come from starches and sugars, and they are not very healthy. They can give you a quick energy boost and may be necessary at some points in the day depending on how much you exercise, but they shouldn't make up the bulk of your diet.
  - **Proteins:** Proteins are extremely important in ensuring your body has enough energy to get through the day. If you're exercising regularly, you need to eat enough protein to help your muscle rebuild after you work out, too.
- Choose healthy sources of protein that come from lean animal meats whenever possible. Poultry, fish, and eggs are good options.
- You can also get protein from some plants, such as mushrooms or broccoli.
  - **Fat:** It's easy to think that all fats should be avoided, but this simply isn't the case. Fat is a nutrient, just like all the others on this list, and you shouldn't cut it out of your diet altogether. You should, however, try to choose healthy sources of fat whenever possible.
- Lean fat sources are best. It's ideal to stick to fish and eggs as well as plant sources of fats (such as avocado) whenever possible.
- Animal fats may be too rich for a diabetic diet. However, some leaner sources of animal fats, such as poultry, can be useful.

- **Other Essential Nutrients**
  - **Sodium:** Eating too much sodium can cause high blood pressure in diabetics (and in non-diabetics as well). However, your body needs some sodium in order to function properly.
  - **Potassium:** Potassium is one of the nutrients your body requires in order to produce insulin. When your potassium is too low, you will feel the effects of your diabetes more fully. Eating enough potassium from healthy plant sources is a great way to improve your overall wellbeing when you are diabetic.
  - **Magnesium:** When your body is resistant to insulin, it may also have low magnesium levels. You should focus on foods that are high in magnesium to keep yourself as well as possible.
  - **Calcium:** Calcium comes from milk, eggs, and several plant sources. You need plenty of calcium in your diet every day, so be sure to stock up on these healthy foods.

- **Carb Counting**
  - Carb counting is one of the most common methods of managing diabetes through your diet. To carb count, you should check the number of carbohydrate grams in every food you eat and then match your insulin dosage to that number.
  - Individuals who use an insulin pump should use an insulin-to-carb ratio to determine their dosage after every meal.
  - Those who are not on insulin but still want to count carbs to help manage their diabetes can do so by using carbohydrate choices instead. Each choice should account for roughly 15 grams of carbohydrates, and sticking to this plan can help you manage your diabetes and prevent the need for insulin injections too.
  - Others use the plate method to make sure they aren't eating too

many carbs at a given meal. To do this, make sure the foods you eat that contain carbs make up no more than one quarter of your plate.

o The number of carbs you need in a meal or in a day will depend on your individual diabetes diagnosis, your age, your weight, and any other health conditions you may be dealing with at the same time. For this reason, it's necessary to work with a medical professional to make sure you're eating the right amount of carbs and other nutrients every day.

- **How to Read Labels**

o Learning how to read labels is crucial in managing your diabetes through your diet. Check the labels first for ingredients that are known for being good for your heart, and learn how to recognize fats and oils that are unhealthy.

o Check for sugar content, but don't forget to check for carbohydrate content as well. Carbohydrates include natural sugar, complex carbs, and fiber, all of which are important to consider in your diabetic diet.

o Remember that sugar-free doesn't necessarily mean healthy. Some sugar-free foods are still very high in carbs, calories, or fat content.

o Fat-free isn't always healthy either. Check labels to find monounsaturated and polyunsaturated fats, which are healthier than saturated and trans fats.

- **Foods to Eat**

This list does not contain every food you can eat on a diabetic diet, but it can help you get started understand what to focus on when meal planning.

- Berries and citrus. Berries are very good for you because they contain lots of antioxidants. They also include vitamin C, potassium, and manganese, and some also contain vitamin K. Citrus also contains antioxidants and lots of vitamin C as well as plenty of potassium.

- Beans. Beans are packed with protein and are great at reducing hunger. They are a healthy starch that also include complex carbs, which are better for you than other types of carbs. Beans can also help you regulate your cholesterol and get enough magnesium in your diet. Just be sure to prepare beans that do not have salt added.

- Whole grains. Instead of refined or processed grains, stick with whole grains. They are high in fiber content and contain healthy carbohydrates. Additionally, since they take longer for your body to digest, they help balance your blood glucose levels over time.

- Leafy greens. You should eat some leafy greens every day whenever possible. They are very healthy and contain tons of nutrients, including calcium, potassium, vitamin A, and other vitamins. Leafy greens also contain antioxidants and are helpful in regulating your digestive system at the same time as they improve your blood glucose levels.

- Fatty fish. Pack your diet with protein sourced from fatty fish whenever possible. Fatty fish contains omega-3 fatty acids, which are important for your brain and heart. They also contain healthy fats.

- Sweet potatoes. Sweet potatoes have healthy fiber as well as vitamin C, vitamin A, and lots of potassium. They don't increase your blood sugar like starchy white potatoes do, and they can be prepared in a lot of different tasty methods to keep them interesting as well.

- **Foods to Avoid**

Below, you'll find some of the most common foods you should avoid when you are diabetic.

- Foods that are very high in carbs. You do need enough carbs every day to help balance your blood sugar, but high carbs can throw off your blood glucose more than help it. Work to make sure you're managing your carbs appropriately.
- Saturated and trans fats. These are usually found in fried, baked, and oily foods like French fries or donuts. They are "bad fats" and should be avoided.
- Drinks with sugar or with sugar substitutes. Soda, energy drinks, sweet tea, or very sugary coffee drinks should be avoided.
- Overly salty food. Too much salt (or sodium) in your food can cause your blood pressure to rise to dangerously high levels. Everyone, diabetic or not, should aim for 2300mg of sodium per day or, ideally, less.
- Processed sugar. Sometimes also called refined sugar, this ingredient is usually found in desserts. It is not the same as sugar found in milk or fruit.
- Alcohol in larger quantities. It's usually okay to have one drink

with a meal, but too much alcohol should be avoided as well.

- Processed or refined grains. Just like refined sugar, refined grain can contain too much sugar or carb content and negatively affect your blood glucose.
- Certain plant starches and sugars. Potatoes, melons, pineapple, and pumpkin all contain more starch and sugar than is healthy for a diabetic diet, except in extreme moderation.

Watching What You Eat

This section can help you better understand how to watch what you eat and which foods to pay extra attention to when planning your meals for the week.

- **Portion Control**
  - Portion control is by far the most important method of controlling your diabetes symptoms through your diet. By watching your portions, you can improve your overall health and wellbeing, sometimes without the use of medication at all.
  - Always read labels to make sure you're eating the proper serving size of any food or ingredient.
  - Invest in a food scale and use it to weigh proper portions. Eyeballing your portion sizes can quickly lead to overdoing it.
  - Use smaller plates to help yourself feel like you're getting larger portions. This can also help you manage your portions by simply not loading up a larger plate with a lot of extra food.
  - Be careful when going out to eat, especially at buffets. Consider asking for a to-go bag before you ever start eating, so you can make

sure to save some for later.

- **Alcohol**

  o Alcohol contains sugars, carbs, and calories, all of which may factor into your diabetic diet. Since liquid carbs are absorbed fast, they don't really make a difference in balancing your blood sugar, but the calories present in alcohol still add up.

  o Many medications used to treat diabetes interact badly with alcohol. Drinking alcohol with these medications can lead to low blood sugar, which can be very dangerous.

  o It's usually okay to have one drink with a meal when you are diabetic. However, multiple drinks in a day, or drinks on an empty stomach, should be avoided.

- **Sugar Substitutes**

  o It can be tempting to use sugar substitutes as part of your diabetic diet. However, most of the time, it's better to skip these unless you're sure you can choose one of the healthier options. Some sugar substitutes can actually increase your risk of worsening your diabetes, especially when consumed for a long time.

  o Some of the healthiest sugar substitutes available are stevia, monk fruit, coconut palm sugar, and date sugar. These all come from natural sources and some even contain antioxidants that can help you stay healthier.

  ▪ Stevia increases your body's insulin production and improves your blood sugar levels.

  ▪ Monk fruit is a sweetener made from pressed or extracted monk fruit, making it a good, natural way to sweeten your food.

  ▪ Coconut palm sugar and date sugar are made of dried and ground natural ingredients. Date sugar is also a good source of fiber.

o Sugar alcohols are types of sweeteners that can be found naturally in some plants, although most are made from chemicals. These include xylitol, sorbitol, and sucralose, among others. Sweeteners like Sweet-N-Low or Splenda contain these sugar alcohols.

▪ Although sugar alcohols are synthetic, they are actually better for you than some other artificial sweeteners. Your body can metabolize them without the use of insulin, and they can also be partially digested. Both of these factors cut down on risks associated with using sugar alcohols as sweeteners.

o Of the sugar substitutes on the market, stevia is the healthiest option for most diabetic individuals.

Important Tips for Managing Diabetes

For now, we'll leave this chapter with some important tips that can help you manage your diabctcs diagnosis. These tips are necessary to keep in mind when working toward a healthier method of living with your diagnosis.

- Always work with a trusted doctor, and consider working with a nutritionist as well. Medical professionals can give you the best advice about your specific needs.
- Eat well-balanced meals and don't be afraid to choose healthy snacks if you get hungry in between meals.
- Always plan your meals ahead of time.
- Go grocery shopping with a list to avoid purchasing unhealthy snack foods.
- Get enough exercise for your age, weight, and other health conditions.
- Hydrate, hydrate, hydrate! Drink plenty of water every day.
- If you are on insulin or other medication, always take it as directed by your doctor, and make sure you have extra doses with you at all times.

Chapter 3 Breakfasts

Egg Bites with Sausage and Peppers

Prep time: 5 minutes | Cook time: 15 minutes | Serves 7

4 large eggs

¼ cup vegan cream cheese (such as Tofutti brand) or cream cheese

¼ teaspoon fine sea salt

¼ teaspoon freshly ground black pepper

3 ounces lean turkey sausage, cooked and crumbled, or 1 vegetarian sausage (such as Beyond Meat brand), cooked and diced

½ red bell pepper, seeded and chopped

2 green onions, white and green parts, minced, plus more for garnish (optional)

¼ cup vegan cheese shreds or shredded sharp Cheddar cheese

1. In a blender, combine the eggs, cream cheese, salt, and pepper. Blend on medium speed for about 20 seconds, just until combined. Add the sausage, bell pepper, and green onions and pulse for 1 second once or twice. You want to mix in the solid ingredients without grinding them up very much. 2. Pour 1 cup water into the Instant Pot. Generously grease a 7-cup egg-bite mold or seven 2-ounce silicone baking cups with butter or coconut oil, making sure to coat each cup well. Place the prepared mold or cups on a long-handled silicone steam rack. (If you don't have the long-handled rack, use the wire metal steam rack and a homemade sling) 3. Pour ¼ cup of the egg mixture into each prepared mold or cup. Holding the handles of the steam rack, carefully lower the egg bites into the pot. 4. Secure the lid and set the Pressure Release to Sealing. Select the Steam setting and set the cooking time for 8 minutes at low pressure. (The pot will take about 5 minutes to come up to pressure before the cooking program begins.) 5. When the cooking program ends, let the pressure release naturally for 5 minutes, then move the Pressure Release to Venting to release any remaining steam. Open the pot. The egg muffins will have puffed up quite a bit during cooking, but they will deflate and settle as they cool. Wearing heat-resistant mitts, grasp the handles of the steam rack and carefully lift the egg bites out of the pot. Sprinkle the egg bites with the cheese, then let them cool for about 5 minutes, until the cheese has fully melted and you are able to handle the mold or cups comfortably. 6. Pull the sides of the egg mold or cups away from the egg bites, running a butter knife around

the edge of each bite to loosen if necessary. Transfer the egg bites to plates, garnish with more green onions (if desired), and serve warm. To store, let cool to room temperature, transfer to an airtight container, and refrigerate for up to 3 days; reheat gently in the microwave for about 1 minute before serving.

Per Serving

calories: 112 | fat: 8g | protein: 8g | carbs: 3g | sugars: 0g | fiber: 0g | sodium: 297mg

Smoked Salmon and Asparagus Quiche Cups

Prep time: 15 minutes | Cook time: 15 minutes | Serves 2

Nonstick cooking spray
4 asparagus spears, cut into ½-inch pieces
2 tablespoons finely chopped onion
3 ounces (85 g) smoked salmon (skinless and boneless), chopped
3 large eggs
2 tablespoons 2% milk
¼ teaspoon dried dill
Pinch ground white pepper

1. Pour 1½ cups of water into the electric pressure cooker and insert a wire rack or trivet. 2. Lightly spray the bottom and sides of the ramekins with nonstick cooking spray. Divide the asparagus, onion, and salmon between the ramekins. 3. In a measuring cup with a spout, whisk together the eggs, milk, dill, and white pepper. Pour half of the egg mixture into each ramekin. Loosely cover the ramekins with aluminum foil. 4. Carefully place the ramekins inside the pot on the rack. 5. Close and lock the lid of the pressure cooker. Set the valve to sealing. 6. Cook on high pressure for 15 minutes. 7. When the cooking is complete, hit Cancel and quick release the pressure. 8. Once the pin drops, unlock and remove the lid. 9. Carefully remove the ramekins from the pot. Cool, covered, for 5 minutes. 10. Run a small silicone spatula or a knife around the edge of each ramekin. Invert each quiche onto a small plate and serve.

Per Serving

calories: 180 | fat: 9g | protein: 20g | carbs: 3g | sugars: 1g | fiber: 1g | sodium: 646mg

Breakfast Farro with Berries and Walnuts

Prep time: 8 minutes | Cook time: 10 minutes | Serves 6

1 cup farro, rinsed and drained
1 cup unsweetened almond milk
¼ teaspoon kosher salt
½ teaspoon pure vanilla extract
1 teaspoon ground cinnamon
1 tablespoon pure maple syrup
1½ cups fresh blueberries, raspberries, or strawberries (or a combination)
6 tablespoons chopped walnuts

1. In the electric pressure cooker, combine the farro, almond milk, 1 cup of water, salt, vanilla, cinnamon, and maple syrup. 2. Close and lock the lid. Set the valve to sealing. 3. Cook on high pressure for 10 minutes. 4. When the cooking is complete, allow the pressure to release naturally for 10 minutes, then quick release any remaining pressure. Hit Cancel. 5. Once the pin drops, unlock and remove the lid. 6. Stir the farro. Spoon into bowls and top each serving with ¼ cup of berries and 1 tablespoon of walnuts.

Per Serving

Calorie: 189 | fat: 5g | protein: 5g | carbs: 32g | sugars: 6g | fiber: 3g | sodium: 111mg

Poached Eggs

Prep time: 5 minutes | Cook time: 5 minutes | Serves 4

Nonstick cooking spray
4 large eggs

1. Lightly spray 4 cups of a 7-count silicone egg bite mold with nonstick cooking spray. Crack each egg into a sprayed cup. 2. Pour 1 cup of water into the electric pressure cooker. Place the egg bite mold on the wire rack and carefully lower it into the pot. 3. Close and lock the lid of the pressure cooker. Set the valve to sealing. 4. Cook on high pressure for 5 minutes. 5. When the cooking is complete, hit Cancel and quick release the pressure. 6. Once the pin drops, unlock and remove the lid. 7. Run a small rubber spatula or spoon around each egg and

carefully remove it from the mold. The white should be cooked, but the yolk should be runny. 8. Serve immediately.

Per Serving

calories: 78 | fat: 5g | protein: 6g | carbs: 1g | sugars: 0g | fiber: 0g | sodium: 62mg

Blueberry Oat Mini Muffins

Prep time: 12 minutes | Cook time: 10 minutes | Serves 7

½ cup rolled oats

¼ cup whole wheat pastry flour or white whole wheat flour

½ tablespoon baking powder

½ teaspoon ground cardamom or ground cinnamon

⅛ teaspoon kosher salt

2 large eggs

½ cup plain Greek yogurt

2 tablespoons pure maple syrup

2 teaspoons extra-virgin olive oil

½ teaspoon vanilla extract

½ cup frozen blueberries (preferably small wild blueberries)

1. In a large bowl, stir together the oats, flour, baking powder, cardamom, and salt. 2. In a medium bowl, whisk together the eggs, yogurt, maple syrup, oil, and vanilla. 3. Add the egg mixture to oat mixture and stir just until combined. Gently fold in the blueberries. 4. Scoop the batter into each cup of the egg bite mold. 5. Pour 1 cup of water into the electric pressure cooker. Place the egg bite mold on the wire rack and carefully lower it into the pot. 6. Close and lock the lid of the pressure cooker. Set the valve to sealing. 7. Cook on high pressure for 10 minutes. 8. When the cooking is complete, allow the pressure to release naturally for 10 minutes, then quick release any remaining pressure. Hit Cancel. 9. Lift the wire rack out of the pot and place on a cooling rack for 5 minutes. Invert the mold onto the cooling rack to release the muffins. 10. Serve the muffins warm or refrigerate or freeze.

Per Serving

calories: 117 | fat: 4g | protein: 5g | carbs: 15g | sugars: 4g | fiber: 2g | sodium: 89mg

Southwestern Egg Casserole

Prep time: 10 minutes | Cook time: 20 minutes | Serves 12

1 cup water
2½ cups egg substitute
½ cup flour
1 teaspoon baking powder
⅛ teaspoon salt
⅛ teaspoon pepper
2 cups fat-free cottage cheese
1½ cups shredded 75%-less-fat sharp cheddar cheese
¼ cup no-trans-fat tub margarine, melted
2 (4-ounce) cans chopped green chilies

1. Place the steaming rack into the bottom of the inner pot and pour in 1 cup of water. 2. Grease a round spring form pan that will fit into the inner pot of the Instant Pot. 3. Combine the egg substitute, flour, baking powder, salt and pepper in a mixing bowl. It will be lumpy. 4. Stir in the cheese, margarine, and green chilies then pour into the spring form pan. 5. Place the spring form pan onto the steaming rack, close the lid, and secure to the locking position. Be sure the vent is turned to sealing. Set for 20 minutes on Manual at high pressure. 6. Let the pressure release naturally. 7. Carefully remove the spring form pan with the handles of the steaming rack and allow to stand 10 minutes before cutting and serving.

Per Serving
calories: 130 | fat: 4g | protein: 14g | carbs: 9g | sugars: 1g | fiber: 1g | sodium: 450mg

Cynthia's Yogurt

Prep time: 10 minutes | Cook time: 8 hours | Serves 16

1 gallon low-fat milk
¼ cup low-fat plain yogurt with active cultures

1. Pour milk into the inner pot of the Instant Pot. 2. Lock lid, move vent to sealing, and press the yogurt button. Press Adjust till it reads "boil." 3. When boil cycle is

complete (about 1 hour), check the temperature. It should be at 185°F. If it's not, use the Sauté function to warm to 185. 4. After it reaches 185°F, unplug Instant Pot, remove inner pot, and cool. You can place on cooling rack and let it slowly cool. If in a hurry, submerge the base of the pot in cool water. Cool milk to 110°F. 5. When mixture reaches 110, stir in the ¼ cup of yogurt. Lock the lid in place and move vent to sealing. 6. Press Yogurt. Use the Adjust button until the screen says 8:00. This will now incubate for 8 hours. 7. After 8 hours (when the cycle is finished), chill yogurt, or go immediately to straining in step 8. 8. After chilling, or following the 8 hours, strain the yogurt using a nut milk bag. This will give it the consistency of Greek yogurt.

Per Serving

calories: 141 | fat: 5g | protein: 10g | carbs: 14g | sugars: 1g | fiber: 0g | sodium: 145mg

Coddled Huevos Rancheros

Prep time: 5 minutes | Cook time: 10 minutes | Serves 2

2 teaspoons unsalted butter

4 large eggs

1 cup drained cooked black beans, or two-thirds 15-ounce can black beans, rinsed and drained

Two 7-inch corn or whole-wheat tortillas, warmed

½ cup chunky tomato salsa (such as Pace brand)

2 cups shredded romaine lettuce

1 tablespoon chopped fresh cilantro

2 tablespoons grated Cotija cheese

1. Pour 1 cup water into the Instant Pot and place a long-handled silicone steam rack into the pot. (If you don't have the long-handled rack, use the wire metal steam rack and a homemade sling) 2. Coat each of four 4-ounce ramekins with ½ teaspoon butter. Crack an egg into each ramekin. Place the ramekins on the steam rack in the pot. 3. Secure the lid and set the Pressure Release to Sealing. Select the Steam setting and set the cooking time for 3 minutes at low pressure. (The pot will take about 5 minutes to come up to pressure before the cooking program begins.) 4. While the eggs are cooking, in a small saucepan over low heat, warm the beans for about 5 minutes, stirring occasionally. Cover the saucepan and remove from the heat. (Alternatively, warm the beans in a covered bowl in a

microwave for 1 minute. Leave the beans covered until ready to serve.) 5. When the cooking program ends, let the pressure release naturally for 5 minutes, then move the Pressure Release to Venting to release any remaining steam. Open the pot and, wearing heat-resistant mitts, grasp the handles of the steam rack and carefully lift it out of the pot. 6. Place a warmed tortilla on each plate and spoon ½ cup of the beans onto each tortilla. Run a knife around the inside edge of each ramekin to loosen the egg and unmold two eggs onto the beans on each tortilla. Spoon the salsa over the eggs and top with the lettuce, cilantro, and cheese. Serve right away.

Per Serving

Calorie: 112 | fat: 8g | protein: 8g | carbs: 3g | sugars: 0g | fiber: 0g | sodium: 297mg

Potato-Bacon Gratin

Prep time: 20 minutes | Cook time: 40 minutes | Serves 8

1 tablespoon olive oil
6-ounces bag fresh spinach
1 clove garlic, minced
4 large potatoes, peeled or unpeeled, divided
6-ounces Canadian bacon slices, divided
5-ounces reduced-fat grated Swiss cheddar, divided
1 cup lower-sodium, lower-fat chicken broth

1. Set the Instant Pot to Sauté and pour in the olive oil. Cook the spinach and garlic in olive oil just until spinach is wilted (5 minutes or less). Turn off the instant pot. 2. Cut potatoes into thin slices about ¼" thick. 3. In a springform pan that will fit into the inner pot of your Instant Pot, spray it with nonstick spray then layer ⅓ the potatoes, half the bacon, ⅓ the cheese, and half the wilted spinach. 4. Repeat layers ending with potatoes. Reserve ⅓ cheese for later. 5. Pour chicken broth over all. 6. Wipe the bottom of your Instant Pot to soak up any remaining oil, then add in 2 cups of water and the steaming rack. Place the springform pan on top. 7. Close the lid and secure to the locking position. Be sure the vent is turned to sealing. Set for 35 minutes on Manual at high pressure. 8. Perform a quick release. 9. Top with the remaining cheese, then allow to stand 10 minutes before removing from the Instant Pot, cutting and serving.

Per Serving

calories: 220 | fat: 7g | protein: 14g | carbs: 28g | sugars: 2g | fiber: 3g | sodium: 415mg

Breakfast Millet with Nuts and Strawberries

Prep time: 0 minutes | Cook time: 30 minutes | Serves 8

2 tablespoons coconut oil or unsalted butter
1½ cups millet
2⅔ cups water
½ teaspoon fine sea salt
1 cup unsweetened almond milk or other nondairy milk
1 cup chopped toasted pecans, almonds, or peanuts
4 cups sliced strawberries

1. Select the Sauté setting on the Instant Pot and melt the oil. Add the millet and cook for 4 minutes, until aromatic. Stir in the water and salt, making sure all of the grains are submerged in the liquid. 2. Secure the lid and set the Pressure Release to Sealing. Press the Cancel button to reset the cooking program, then select the Porridge, Pressure Cook, or Manual setting and set the cooking time for 12 minutes at high pressure. (The pot will take about 10 minutes to come up to pressure before the cooking program begins.) 3. When the cooking program ends, let the pressure release naturally for 10 minutes, then move the Pressure Release to Venting to release any remaining steam. Open the pot and use a fork to fluff and stir the millet. 4. Spoon the millet into bowls and top each serving with 2 tablespoons of the almond milk, then sprinkle with the nuts and top with the strawberries. Serve warm.

Per Serving
calories: 270 | fat: 13g | protein: 6g | carbs: 35g | sugars: 4g | fiber: 6g | sodium: 151mg

Cinnamon French Toast

Prep time: 10 minutes | Cook time: 20 minutes | Serves 8

3 eggs

2 cups low-fat milk

2 tablespoons maple syrup

15 drops liquid stevia

2 teaspoons vanilla extract

2 teaspoons cinnamon

Pinch salt

16-ounces whole wheat bread, cubed and left out overnight to go stale

1½ cups water

1. In a medium bowl, whisk together the eggs, milk, maple syrup, Stevia, vanilla, cinnamon, and salt. Stir in the cubes of whole wheat bread. 2. You will need a 7-inch round baking pan for this. Spray the inside with nonstick spray, then pour the bread mixture into the pan. 3. Place the trivet in the bottom of the inner pot, then pour in the water. 4. Make foil sling and insert it onto the trivet. Carefully place the 7-inch pan on top of the foil sling/trivet. 5. Secure the lid to the locked position, then make sure the vent is turned to sealing. 6. Press the Manual button and use the "+/-" button to set the Instant Pot for 20 minutes. 7. When cook time is up, let the Instant Pot release naturally for 5 minutes, then quick release the rest

Per Serving

calories: 75 | fat: 3g | protein: 4g | carbs: 7g | sugars: 6g | fiber: 0g | sodium: 74mg

Tropical Steel Cut Oats

Prep time: 5 minutes | Cook time: 5 minutes | Serves 4

1 cup steel cut oats
1 cup unsweetened almond milk
2 cups coconut water or water
¾ cup frozen chopped peaches
¾ cup frozen mango chunks
1 (2-inch) vanilla bean, scraped (seeds and pod)
Ground cinnamon
¼ cup chopped unsalted macadamia nuts

1. In the electric pressure cooker, combine the oats, almond milk, coconut water, peaches, mango chunks, and vanilla bean seeds and pod. Stir well. 2. Close and lock the lid of the pressure cooker. Set the valve to sealing. 3. Cook on high pressure for 5 minutes. 4. When the cooking is complete, allow the pressure to release naturally for 10 minutes, then quick release any remaining pressure. Hit Cancel. 5. Once the pin drops, unlock and remove the lid. 6. Discard the vanilla bean pod and stir well. 7. Spoon the oats into 4 bowls. Top each serving with a sprinkle of cinnamon and 1 tablespoon of the macadamia nuts.

Per Serving

calories: 127 | fat: 7g | protein: 2g | carbs: 14g | sugars: 8g | fiber: 3g | sodium: 167mg

Gouda Egg Casserole with Canadian Bacon

Prep time: 12 minutes | Cook time: 20 minutes | Serves 4

Nonstick cooking spray
1 slice whole grain bread, toasted
½ cup shredded smoked Gouda cheese
3 slices Canadian bacon, chopped
6 large eggs
¼ cup half-and-half
¼ teaspoon kosher salt
¼ teaspoon freshly ground black pepper
¼ teaspoon dry mustard

1. Spray a 6-inch cake pan with cooking spray, or if the pan is nonstick, skip this step. If you don't have a 6-inch cake pan, any bowl or pan that fits inside your pressure cooker should work. 2. Crumble the toast into the bottom of the pan. Sprinkle with the cheese and Canadian bacon. 3. In a medium bowl, whisk together the eggs, half-and-half, salt, pepper, and dry mustard. 4. Pour the egg mixture into the pan. Loosely cover the pan with aluminum foil. 5. Pour 1½ cups water into the electric pressure cooker and insert a wire rack or trivet. Place the covered pan on top of the rack. 6. Close and lock the lid of the pressure cooker. Set the valve to sealing. 7. Cook on high pressure for 20 minutes. 8. When the cooking is complete, hit Cancel and quick release the pressure. 9. Once the pin drops, unlock and remove the lid. 10. Carefully transfer the pan from the pressure cooker to a cooling rack and let it sit for 5 minutes. 11. Cut into 4 wedges and serve.

Greek Frittata with Peppers, Kale, and Feta

Prep time: 5 minutes | Cook time: 45 minutes | Serves 6

8 large eggs
½ cup plain 2 percent Greek yogurt
Fine sea salt
Freshly ground black pepper
2 cups firmly packed finely shredded kale or baby kale leaves
One 12-ounce jar roasted red peppers, drained and cut into ¼ by 2-inch strips
2 green onions, white and green parts, thinly sliced
1 tablespoon chopped fresh dill
⅓ cup crumbled feta cheese
6 cups loosely packed mixed baby greens
¾ cup cherry or grape tomatoes, halved
2 tablespoons extra-virgin olive oil

1. Pour 1½ cups water into the Instant Pot. Lightly butter a 7-cup round heatproof glass dish or coat with nonstick cooking spray. 2. In a bowl, whisk together the eggs, yogurt, ¼ teaspoon salt, and ¼ teaspoon pepper until well blended, then stir in the kale, roasted peppers, green onions, dill, and feta cheese. 3. Pour the egg mixture into the prepared dish and cover tightly with aluminum foil. Place the dish on a long-handled silicone steam rack, then, holding the

handles of the steam rack, lower it into the Instant Pot. (If you don't have the long-handled rack, use the wire metal steam rack and a homemade sling) 4. Secure the lid and set the Pressure Release to Sealing. Select the Pressure Cook or Manual setting and set the cooking time for 30 minutes at high pressure. (The pot will take about 15 minutes to come up to pressure before the cooking program begins.) 5. When the cooking program ends, let the pressure release naturally for 10 minutes, then move the Pressure Release to Venting to release any remaining steam. Open the pot and let the frittata sit for a minute or two, until it deflates and settles into its dish. Then, wearing heat-resistant mitts, grasp the handles of the steam rack and lift it out of the pot. Uncover the dish, taking care not to get burned by the steam or to drip condensation onto the frittata. Let the frittata sit for 10 minutes, giving it time to reabsorb any liquid and set up. 6. In a medium bowl, toss together the mixed greens, tomatoes, and olive oil. Taste and adjust the seasoning with salt and pepper, if needed. 7. Cut the frittata into six wedges and serve warm, with the salad alongside.

Per Serving

calories: 227 | fat: 13g | protein: 18g | carbs: 8g | sugars: 2g | fiber: 1g | sodium: 153mg

Grain-Free Apple Cinnamon Cake

Prep time: 10 minutes | Cook time: 50 minutes | Serves 8

2 cups almond flour
½ cup Lakanto Monkfruit Sweetener Golden
1½ teaspoons ground cinnamon
1 teaspoon baking powder
½ teaspoon fine sea salt
½ cup plain 2 percent Greek yogurt
2 large eggs
½ teaspoon pure vanilla extract
1 small apple, chopped into small pieces

1. Pour 1 cup water into the Instant Pot. Line the base of a 7 by 3-inch round cake pan with parchment paper. Butter the sides of the pan and the parchment or coat with nonstick cooking spray. 2. In a medium bowl, whisk together the almond flour, sweetener, cinnamon, baking powder, and salt. In a smaller bowl, whisk

together the yogurt, eggs, and vanilla until no streaks of yolk remain. Add the wet mixture to the dry mixture and stir just until the dry ingredients are evenly moistened, then fold in the apple. The batter will be very thick. 3. Transfer the batter to the prepared pan and, using a rubber spatula, spread it in an even layer. Cover the pan tightly with aluminum foil. Place the pan on a long-handled silicone steam rack, then, holding the handles of the steam rack, lower it into the Instant Pot. (If you don't have the long-handled rack, use the wire metal steam rack and a homemade sling) 4. Secure the lid and set the Pressure Release to Sealing. Select the Cake, Pressure Cook, or Manual setting and set the cooking time for 40 minutes at high pressure. (The pot will take about 10 minutes to come up to pressure before the cooking program begins.) 5. When the cooking program ends, let the pressure release naturally for 10 minutes, then move the Pressure Release to Venting to release any remaining steam. Open the pot and, wearing heat-resistant mitts, grasp the handles of the steam rack and lift it out of the pot. Uncover the pan, taking care not to get burned by the steam or to drip condensation onto the cake. Let the cake cool in the pan on a cooling rack for about 5 minutes. 6. Run a butter knife around the edge of the pan to loosen the cake from the pan sides. Invert the cake onto the rack, lift off the pan, and peel off the parchment. Let cool for 15 minutes, then invert the cake onto a serving plate. Cut into eight wedges and serve.

Per Serving

calories: 219 | fat: 16g | protein: 9g | carbs: 20g | sugars: 8g | fiber: 16g | sodium: 154mg

Chapter 4 Snacks and Appetizers

Corn on the Cob

Prep time: 5 minutes | Cook time: 12 to 15 minutes | Serves 4

2 large ears fresh corn
Olive oil for misting
Salt, to taste (optional)

1. Shuck corn, remove silks, and wash. 2. Cut or break each ear in half crosswise. 3. Spray corn with olive oil. 4. Air fry at 390°F (199°C) for 12 to 15 minutes or until browned as much as you like. 5. Serve plain or with coarsely ground salt.

Southern Boiled Peanuts

Prep time: 5 minutes | Cook time: 1 hour 20 minutes | Makes 8 cups

1 pound raw jumbo peanuts in the shell
3 tablespoons fine sea salt

1. Remove the inner pot from the Instant Pot and add the peanuts to it. Cover the peanuts with water and use your hands to agitate them, loosening any dirt. Drain the peanuts in a colander, rinse out the pot, and return the peanuts to it. Return the inner pot to the Instant Pot housing. 2. Add the salt and 9 cups water to the pot and stir to dissolve the salt. Select a salad plate just small enough to fit inside the pot and set it on top of the peanuts to weight them down, submerging them all in the water. 3. Secure the lid and set the Pressure Release to Sealing. Select the Steam setting and set the cooking time for 1 hour at low pressure. (The pot will take about 20 minutes to come up to pressure before the cooking program begins.) 4. When the cooking program ends, let the pressure release naturally (this will take about 1 hour). Open the pot and, wearing heat-resistant mitts, remove the inner pot from the housing. Let the peanuts cool to room temperature in the brine (this will take about 1½ hours). 5. Serve at room temperature or chilled. Transfer the peanuts with their brine to an airtight container and refrigerate for up to 1 week.
Per Serving

calories: 306 | fat: 17g | protein: 26g | carbs: 12g | sugars: 2g | fiber: 4g | sodium: 303mg

Ground Turkey Lettuce Cups

Prep time: 5 minutes | Cook time: 30 minutes | Serves 8

3 tablespoons water

2 tablespoons soy sauce, tamari, or coconut aminos

3 tablespoons fresh lime juice

2 teaspoons Sriracha, plus more for serving

2 tablespoons cold-pressed avocado oil

2 teaspoons toasted sesame oil

4 garlic cloves, minced

1-inch piece fresh ginger, peeled and minced

2 carrots, diced

2 celery stalks, diced

1 yellow onion, diced

2 pounds 93 percent lean ground turkey

½ teaspoon fine sea salt

Two 8-ounce cans sliced water chestnuts, drained and chopped

1 tablespoon cornstarch

2 hearts romaine lettuce or 2 heads butter lettuce, leaves separated

½ cup roasted cashews (whole or halves and pieces), chopped

1 cup loosely packed fresh cilantro leaves

1. In a small bowl, combine the water, soy sauce, 2 tablespoons of the lime juice, and the Sriracha and mix well. Set aside. 2. Select the Sauté setting on the Instant Pot and heat the avocado oil, sesame oil, garlic, and ginger for 2 minutes, until the garlic is bubbling but not browned. Add the carrots, celery, and onion and sauté for about 3 minutes, until the onion begins to soften. 3. Add the turkey and salt and sauté, using a wooden spoon or spatula to break up the meat as it cooks, for about 5 minutes, until cooked through and no streaks of pink remain. Add the water chestnuts and soy sauce mixture and stir to combine, working quickly so not too much steam escapes. 4. Secure the lid and set the Pressure Release to Sealing. Press the Cancel button to reset the cooking program, then select the Pressure Cook or Manual setting and set the cooking time for 5 minutes at high pressure. (The pot will take about 10 minutes to come up to pressure before the cooking program begins.) 5. When the cooking program ends, perform a quick pressure release by moving the Pressure Release to Venting, or let the pressure release naturally. Open the pot. 6. In a small bowl, stir together the remaining 1 tablespoon lime juice and the cornstarch, add the mixture to the pot, and stir to

combine. Press the Cancel button to reset the cooking program, then select the Sauté setting. Let the mixture come to a boil and thicken, stirring often, for about 2 minutes, then press the Cancel button to turn off the pot. 7. Spoon the turkey mixture onto the lettuce leaves and sprinkle the cashews and cilantro on top. Serve right away, with additional Sriracha at the table.

Per Serving

calories: 127 | fat: 7g | protein: 6g | carbs: 10g | sugars: 2g | fiber: 3g | sodium: 392mg

Green Goddess White Bean Dip

Prep time: 1 minutes | Cook time: 45 minutes | Makes 3 cups

1 cup dried navy, great Northern, or cannellini beans

4 cups water

2 teaspoons fine sea salt

3 tablespoons fresh lemon juice

¼ cup extra-virgin olive oil, plus 1 tablespoon

¼ cup firmly packed fresh flat-leaf parsley leaves

1 bunch chives, chopped

Leaves from 2 tarragon sprigs

Freshly ground black pepper

1. Combine the beans, water, and 1 teaspoon of the salt in the Instant Pot and stir to dissolve the salt. 2. Secure the lid and set the Pressure Release to Sealing. Select the Bean/Chili, Pressure Cook, or Manual setting and set the cooking time for 30 minutes at high pressure if using navy or Great Northern beans or 40 minutes at high pressure if using cannellini beans. (The pot will take about 15 minutes to come up to pressure before the cooking program begins.) 3. When the cooking program ends, let the pressure release naturally for 15 minutes, then move the Pressure Release to Venting to release any remaining steam. Open the pot and scoop out and reserve ½ cup of the cooking liquid. Wearing heat-resistant mitts, lift out the inner pot and drain the beans in a colander. 4. In a food processor or blender, combine the beans, ½ cup cooking liquid, lemon juice, ¼ cup olive oil, ½ teaspoon parsley, chives, tarragon, remaining 1 teaspoon salt, and ½ teaspoon pepper. Process or blend on medium speed, stopping to scrape down the sides of the container as needed, for about 1 minute, until the

mixture is smooth. 5. Transfer the dip to a serving bowl. Drizzle with the remaining 1 tablespoon olive oil and sprinkle with a few grinds of pepper. The dip will keep in an airtight container in the refrigerator for up to 1 week. Serve at room temperature or chilled.

Per Serving

Calorie: 70 | fat: 5g | protein: 3g | carbs: 8g | sugars: 1g | fiber: 4g | sodium: 782mg

7-Layer Dip

Prep time: 10 minutes | Cook time: 35 minutes | Serves 6

Cashew Sour Cream
1 cup raw whole cashews, soaked in water to cover for 1 to 2 hours and then drained
½ cup avocado oil
½ cup water
¼ cup fresh lemon juice
2 tablespoons nutritional yeast
1 teaspoon fine sea salt
Beans
½ cup dried black beans
2 cups water
½ teaspoon fine sea salt

½ teaspoon chili powder
¼ teaspoon garlic powder
½ cup grape or cherry tomatoes, halved
1 avocado, diced
¼ cup chopped yellow onion
1 jalapeño chile, sliced
2 tablespoons chopped cilantro
6 ounces baked corn tortilla chips
1 English cucumber, sliced
2 carrots, sliced
6 celery stalks, cut into sticks

1. To make the cashew sour cream: In a blender, combine the cashews, oil, water, lemon juice, nutritional yeast, and salt. Blend on high speed, stopping to scrape down the sides of the container as needed, for about 2 minutes, until very smooth. (The sour cream can be made in advance and stored in an airtight container in the refrigerator for up to 5 days.) 2. To make the beans: Pour 1 cup water into the Instant Pot. In a 1½-quart stainless-steel bowl, combine the beans, the 2 cups water, and salt and stir to dissolve the salt. Place the bowl on a long-handled silicone steam rack, then, holding the handles of the steam rack, lower it into the Instant Pot. (If you don't have the long-handled rack, use the wire metal steam rack and a homemade sling) 3. Secure the lid and set the Pressure Release to Sealing. Select the Bean/Chili, Pressure Cook, or Manual setting and set the cooking time for 25 minutes at high pressure. (The pot will take about 10 minutes

to come up to pressure before the cooking program begins.) 4. When the cooking program ends, let the pressure release naturally for at least 20 minutes, then move the Pressure Release to Venting to release any remaining steam. 5. Place a colander over a bowl. Open the pot and, wearing heat-resistant mitts, lift out the inner pot and drain the beans in the colander. Transfer the liquid captured in the bowl to a measuring cup, and pour the beans into the bowl. Add ¼ cup of the cooking liquid to the beans and, using a potato masher or fork, mash the beans to your desired consistency, adding more cooking liquid as needed. Stir in the chili powder and garlic powder. 6. Using a rubber spatula, spread the black beans in an even layer in a clear-glass serving dish. Spread the cashew sour cream in an even layer on top of the beans. Add layers of the tomatoes, avocado, onion, jalapeño, and cilantro. (At this point, you can cover and refrigerate the assembled dip for up to 1 day.) Serve accompanied with the tortilla chips, cucumber, carrots, and celery on the side.

Per Serving

calories: 259 | fat: 8g | protein: 8g | carbs: 41g | sugars: 3g | fiber: 8g | sodium: 811mg

Hummus with Chickpeas and Tahini Sauce

Prep time: 10 minutes | Cook time: 55 minutes | Makes 4 cups

4 cups water	3 tablespoons fresh lemon juice
1 cup dried chickpeas	1 garlic clove
2½ teaspoons fine sea salt	¼ teaspoon ground cumin
½ cup tahini	

1. Combine the water, chickpeas, and 1 teaspoon of the salt in the Instant Pot and stir to dissolve the salt. 2. Secure the lid and set the Pressure Release to Sealing. Select the Bean/Chili, Pressure Cook, or Manual setting and set the cooking time for 40 minutes at high pressure. (The pot will take about 15 minutes to come up to pressure before the cooking program begins.) 3. When the cooking program ends, let the pressure release naturally for 15 minutes, then move the Pressure Release to Venting to release any remaining steam. 4. Place a colander over a bowl. Open the pot and, wearing heat-resistant mitts, lift out the inner pot and drain the beans in the colander. Return the chickpeas to the inner pot and place it back in the Instant Pot housing on the Keep Warm setting. Reserve the cooking liquid. 5. In a blender or food processor, combine 1 cup of the cooking liquid, the

tahini, lemon juice, garlic, cumin, and 1 teaspoon salt. Blend or process on high speed, stopping to scrape down the sides of the container as needed, for about 30 seconds, until smooth and a little fluffy. Scoop out and set aside ½ cup of this sauce for the topping. 6. Set aside ½ cup of the chickpeas for the topping. Add the remaining chickpeas to the tahini sauce in the blender or food processor along with ½ cup of the cooking liquid and the remaining ½ teaspoon salt. Blend or process on high speed, stopping to scrape down the sides of the container as needed, for about 1 minute, until very smooth. 7. Transfer the hummus to a shallow serving bowl. Spoon the reserved tahini mixture over the top, then sprinkle on the reserved chickpeas. The hummus will keep in an airtight container in the refrigerator for up to 3 days. Serve at room temperature or chilled.

Per Serving

calories: 107 | fat: 5g | protein: 4g | carbs: 10g | sugars: 3g | fiber: 4g | sodium: 753mg

Instant Popcorn

Prep time: 1 minutes | Cook time: 5 minutes | Serves 5

2 tablespoons coconut oil
½ cup popcorn kernels
¼ cup margarine spread, melted, optional
Sea salt to taste

1. Set the Instant Pot to Sauté. 2. Melt the coconut oil in the inner pot, then add the popcorn kernels and stir. 3. Press Adjust to bring the temperature up to high. 4. When the corn starts popping, secure the lid on the Instant Pot. 5. When you no longer hear popping, turn off the Instant Pot, remove the lid, and pour the popcorn into a bowl. 6. Top with the optional melted margarine and season the popcorn with sea salt to your liking.

Per Serving

calories: 161 | fat: 12g | protein: 1g | carbs: 13g | sugars: 0g | fiber: 3g | sodium: 89mg

Candied Pecans

Prep time: 5 minutes | Cook time: 20 minutes | Serves 10

4 cups raw pecans	1 teaspoon cinnamon
1½ teaspoons liquid stevia	¼ teaspoon nutmeg
½ cup plus 1 tablespoon water, divided	⅛ teaspoon ground ginger
1 teaspoon vanilla extract	⅛ teaspoon sea salt

1. Place the raw pecans, liquid stevia, 1 tablespoon water, vanilla, cinnamon, nutmeg, ground ginger, and sea salt into the inner pot of the Instant Pot. 2. Press the Sauté button on the Instant Pot and sauté the pecans and other ingredients until the pecans are soft. 3. Pour in the ½ cup water and secure the lid to the locked position. Set the vent to sealing. 4. Press Manual and set the Instant Pot for 15 minutes. 5. Preheat the oven to 350°F. 6. When cooking time is up, turn off the Instant Pot, then do a quick release. 7. Spread the pecans onto a greased, lined baking sheet. 8. Bake the pecans for 5 minutes or less in the oven, checking on them frequently so they do not burn.

Per Serving

calories: 275 | fat: 28g | protein: 4g | carbs: 6g | sugars: 2g | fiber: 4g | sodium: 20mg

Blackberry Baked Brie

Prep time: 5 minutes | Cook time: 15 minutes | Serves 5

8-ounce round Brie	¼ cup sugar-free blackberry preserves
1 cup water	2 teaspoons chopped fresh mint

1. Slice a grid pattern into the top of the rind of the Brie with a knife. 2. In a 7-inch round baking dish, place the Brie, then cover the baking dish securely with foil. 3. Insert the trivet into the inner pot of the Instant Pot; pour in the water. 4. Make a foil sling and arrange it on top of the trivet. Place the baking dish on top of the trivet and foil sling. 5. Secure the lid to the locked position and turn the vent to sealing. 6. Press Manual and set the Instant Pot for 15 minutes on high pressure. 7. When cooking time is up, turn off the Instant Pot and do a quick release of the pressure. 8. When the valve has dropped, remove the lid, then remove the baking dish. 9. Remove the top rind of the Brie and top with the

preserves. Sprinkle with the fresh mint.

Per Serving

Calorie: 133 | fat: 10g | protein: 8g | carbs: 4g | sugars: 0g | fiber: 0g | sodium: 238mg

Creamy Spinach Dip

Prep time: 13 minutes | Cook time: 5 minutes | Serves 11

8 ounces low-fat cream cheese	¼ teaspoon black pepper
1 cup low-fat sour cream	10 ounces frozen spinach
½ cup finely chopped onion	12 ounces reduced-fat shredded
½ cup no-sodium vegetable broth	Monterey Jack cheese
5 cloves garlic, minced	12 ounces reduced-fat shredded
½ teaspoon salt	Parmesan cheese

1. Add cream cheese, sour cream, onion, vegetable broth, garlic, salt, pepper, and spinach to the inner pot of the Instant Pot. 2. Secure lid, make sure vent is set to sealing, and set to the Bean/Chili setting on high pressure for 5 minutes. 3. When done, do a manual release. 4. Add the cheeses and mix well until creamy and well combined.

Per Serving

Calorie: 274 | fat: 18g | protein: 19g | carbs: 10g | sugars: 3g | fiber: 1g | sodium: 948mg

Spinach and Artichoke Dip

Prep time: 5 minutes | Cook time: 4 minutes | Serves 11

8 ounces low-fat cream cheese	3 cloves of garlic, minced
10-ounce box frozen spinach	1 teaspoon onion powder
½ cup no-sodium chicken broth	16 ounces reduced-fat shredded
14-ounce can artichoke hearts, drained	Parmesan cheese
½ cup low-fat sour cream	8 ounces reduced-fat shredded
½ cup low-fat mayo	mozzarella

1. Put all ingredients in the inner pot of the Instant Pot, except the Parmesan cheese and the mozzarella cheese. 2. Secure the lid and set vent to sealing. Place

on Manual high pressure for 4 minutes. 3. Do a quick release of steam. 4. Immediately stir in the cheeses.

Per Serving

calories: 288 | fat: 18g | protein: 19g | carbs: 15g | sugars: 3g | fiber: 3g | sodium: 1007mg

Creamy Jalapeño Chicken Dip

Prep time: 5 minutes | Cook time: 12 minutes | Serves 10

1 pound boneless chicken breast	8 ounces reduced-fat shredded
8 ounces low-fat cream cheese	cheddar cheese
3 jalapeños, seeded and sliced	¾ cup low-fat sour cream
½ cup water	

1. Place the chicken, cream cheese, jalapeños, and water in the inner pot of the Instant Pot. 2. Secure the lid so it's locked and turn the vent to sealing. 3. Press Manual and set the Instant Pot for 12 minutes on high pressure. 4. When cooking time is up, turn off Instant Pot, do a quick release of the remaining pressure, then remove lid. 5. Shred the chicken between 2 forks, either in the pot or on a cutting board, then place back in the inner pot. 6. Stir in the shredded cheese and sour cream.

Per Serving

calories: 238 | fat: 13g | protein: 24g | carbs: 7g | sugars: 5g | fiber: 1g | sodium: 273mg

Porcupine Meatballs

Prep time: 20 minutes | Cook time: 15 minutes | Serves 8

1 pound ground sirloin or turkey	¼ teaspoon dried basil and/or
½ cup raw brown rice, parboiled	oregano, optional
1 egg	10¾-ounce can reduced-fat
¼ cup finely minced onion	condensed tomato soup
1 or 2 cloves garlic, minced	½ soup can of water

1. Mix all ingredients, except tomato soup and water, in a bowl to combine well. 2. Form into balls about 1½-inch in diameter. 3. Mix tomato soup and water in the inner pot of the Instant Pot, then add the meatballs. 4. Secure the lid and make

sure the vent is turned to sealing. 5. Press the Meat button and set for 15 minutes on high pressure. 6. Allow the pressure to release naturally after cook time is up.

Per Serving

calories: 141 | fat: 2g | protein: 16g | carbs: 14g | sugars: 3g | fiber: 1g | sodium: 176mg

Lemon Artichokes

Prep time: 5 minutes | Cook time: 5 to 15 minutes | Serves 4

4 artichokes	2 tablespoons lemon juice
1 cup water	1 teaspoon salt

1. Wash and trim artichokes by cutting off the stems flush with the bottoms of the artichokes and by cutting ¾–1 inch off the tops. Stand upright in the bottom of the inner pot of the Instant Pot. 2. Pour water, lemon juice, and salt over artichokes. 3. Secure the lid and make sure the vent is set to sealing. On Manual, set the Instant Pot for 15 minutes for large artichokes, 10 minutes for medium artichokes, or 5 minutes for small artichokes. 4. When cook time is up, perform a quick release by releasing the pressure manually.

Per Serving

calories: 60 | fat: 0g | protein: 4g | carbs: 13g | sugars: 1g | fiber: 6g | sodium: 397mg

Chapter 5 Poultry

Pulled BBQ Chicken and Texas-Style Cabbage Slaw

Prep time: 5 minutes | Cook time: 20 minutes | Serves 6

Chicken

1 cup water

¼ teaspoon fine sea salt

3 garlic cloves, peeled

2 bay leaves

2 pounds boneless, skinless chicken thighs (see Note)

Cabbage Slaw

½ head red or green cabbage, thinly sliced

1 red bell pepper, seeded and thinly sliced

2 jalapeño chiles, seeded and cut into narrow strips

2 carrots, julienned

1 large Fuji or Gala apple, julienned

½ cup chopped fresh cilantro

3 tablespoons fresh lime juice

3 tablespoons extra-virgin olive oil

½ teaspoon ground cumin

¼ teaspoon fine sea salt

¾ cup low-sugar or unsweetened barbecue sauce

Cornbread, for serving

1. To make the chicken: Combine the water, salt, garlic, bay leaves, and chicken thighs in the Instant Pot, arranging the chicken in a single layer. 2. Secure the lid and set the Pressure Release to Sealing. Select the Poultry, Pressure Cook, or Manual setting and set the cooking time for 10 minutes at high pressure. (The pot will take about 10 minutes to come up to pressure before the cooking program begins.) 3. To make the slaw: While the chicken is cooking, in a large bowl, combine the cabbage, bell pepper, jalapeños, carrots, apple, cilantro, lime juice, oil, cumin, and salt and toss together until the vegetables and apples are evenly coated. 4. When the cooking program ends, perform a quick pressure release by moving the Pressure Release to Venting, or let the pressure release naturally. Open the pot and, using tongs, transfer the chicken to a cutting board. Using two forks, shred the chicken into bite-size pieces. Wearing heat-resistant mitts, lift out the inner pot and discard the cooking liquid. Return the inner pot to the housing. 5. Return the chicken to the pot and stir in the barbecue sauce. You can serve it right away or heat it for a minute or two on the Sauté setting, then return the pot to its Keep Warm setting until ready to serve. 6. Divide the chicken and slaw evenly among six plates. Serve with wedges of cornbread on the side.
Per Serving

calories: 320 | fat: 14g | protein: 32g | carbs: 18g | sugars: 7g | fiber: 4g | sodium: 386mg

Lemony Chicken Thighs

Prep time: 15 minutes | Cook time: 15 minutes | Serves 3 to 5

1 cup low-sodium chicken bone broth	¼ teaspoon black pepper
5 frozen bone-in chicken thighs	1 teaspoon True Lemon Lemon Pepper
1 small onion, diced	seasoning
5–6 cloves garlic, diced	1 teaspoon parsley flakes
Juice of 1 lemon	¼ teaspoon oregano
2 tablespoons margarine, melted	Rind of 1 lemon
½ teaspoon salt	

1. Add the chicken bone broth into the inner pot of the Instant Pot. 2. Add the chicken thighs. 3. Add the onion and garlic. 4. Pour the fresh lemon juice in with the melted margarine. 5. Add the seasonings. 6. Lock the lid, make sure the vent is at sealing, then press the Poultry button. Set to 15 minutes. 7. When cook time is up, let the pressure naturally release for 3–5 minutes, then manually release the rest. 8. You can place these under the broiler for 2–3 minutes to brown. 9. Plate up and pour some of the sauce over top with fresh grated lemon rind.

Per Serving

calories: 329 | fat: 24g | protein: 26g | carbs: 3g | sugars: 1g | fiber: 0g | sodium: 407mg

32. Garlic Galore Rotisserie Chicken

Prep time: 5 minutes | Cook time: 3 minutes | Serves 4

3-pound whole chicken	or water
2 tablespoons olive oil, divided	2 tablespoons garlic powder
Salt to taste	2 teaspoons onion powder
Pepper to taste	½ teaspoon basil
20–30 cloves fresh garlic, peeled and	½ teaspoon cumin
left whole	½ teaspoon chili powder
1 cup low-sodium chicken stock, broth,	

1. Rub chicken with one tablespoon of the olive oil and sprinkle with salt and

pepper. 2. Place the garlic cloves inside the chicken. Use butcher's twine to secure the legs. 3. Press the Sauté button on the Instant Pot, then add the rest of the olive oil to the inner pot. 4. When the pot is hot, place the chicken inside. You are just trying to sear it, so leave it for about 4 minutes on each side. 5. Remove the chicken and set aside. Place the trivet at the bottom of the inner pot and pour in the chicken stock. 6. Mix together the remaining seasonings and rub them all over the entire chicken. 7. Place the chicken back inside the inner pot, breast-side up, on top of the trivet and secure the lid to the sealing position. 8. Press the Manual button and use the +/- to set it for 25 minutes. 9. When the timer beeps, allow the pressure to release naturally for 15 minutes. If the lid will not open at this point, quick release the remaining pressure and remove the chicken. 10. Let the chicken rest for 5–10 minutes before serving.

Per Serving

calories: 333 | fat: 23g | protein: 24g | carbs: 9g | sugars: 0g | fiber: 1g | sodium: 110mg

Mild Chicken Curry with Coconut Milk

Prep time: 10 minutes | Cook time: 14 minutes | Serves 4 to 6

1 large onion, diced	1 tablespoon curry powder (more if
6 cloves garlic, crushed	you like more flavor)
¼ cup coconut oil	½ teaspoon chili powder
½ teaspoon black pepper	24-ounce can of low-sodium diced or
½ teaspoon turmeric	crushed tomatoes
½ teaspoon paprika	13½-ounce can of light coconut milk
¼ teaspoon cinnamon	(I prefer a brand that has no unwanted
¼ teaspoon cloves	ingredients, like guar gum or sugar)
¼ teaspoon cumin	4 pounds boneless skinless chicken
¼ teaspoon ginger	breasts, cut into chunks
½ teaspoon salt	

1. Sauté onion and garlic in the coconut oil, either with Sauté setting in the inner pot of the Instant Pot or on stove top, then add to pot. 2. Combine spices in a small bowl, then add to the inner pot. 3. Add tomatoes and coconut milk and stir. 4. Add chicken, and stir to coat the pieces with the sauce. 5. Secure the lid and make sure vent is at sealing. Set to Manual mode (or Pressure Cook on newer models) for 14 minutes. 6. Let pressure release naturally (if you're crunched for

time, you can do a quick release). 7. Serve with your favorite sides, and enjoy!

Per Serving

Calorie: 535 | fat: 21g | protein: 71g | carbs: 10g | sugars: 5g | fiber: 2g | sodium: 315mg

Chicken in Wine

Prep time: 10 minutes | Cook time: 12 minutes | Serves 6

2 pounds chicken breasts, trimmed of skin and fat
10¾-ounce can 98% fat-free, reduced-sodium cream of mushroom soup
10¾-ounce can French onion soup
1 cup dry white wine or chicken broth

1. Place the chicken into the Instant Pot. 2. Combine soups and wine. Pour over chicken. 3. Secure the lid and make sure vent is set to sealing. Cook on Manual mode for 12 minutes. 4. When cook time is up, let the pressure release naturally for 5 minutes and then release the rest manually.

Per Serving

calories: 225 | fat: 5g | protein: 35g | carbs: 7g | sugars: 3g | fiber: 1g | sodium: 645mg

Chicken with Spiced Sesame Sauce

Prep time: 20 minutes | Cook time: 8 minutes | Serves 5

2 tablespoons tahini (sesame sauce)
¼ cup water
1 tablespoon low-sodium soy sauce
¼ cup chopped onion
1 teaspoon red wine vinegar
2 teaspoons minced garlic
1 teaspoon shredded ginger root (Microplane works best)
2 pounds chicken breast, chopped into 8 portions

1. Place first seven ingredients in bottom of the inner pot of the Instant Pot. 2. Add coarsely chopped chicken on top. 3. Secure the lid and make sure vent is at sealing. Set for 8 minutes using Manual setting. When cook time is up, let the pressure release naturally for 10 minutes, then perform a quick release. 4. Remove ingredients and shred chicken with fork. Combine with other ingredients in pot for a tasty sandwich filling or sauce.

Per Serving

Calorie: 215 | fat: 7g | protein: 35g | carbs: 2g | sugars: 0g | fiber: 0g | sodium: 178mg

Chicken Reuben Bake

Prep time: 10 minutes | Cook time: 6 to 8 hours | Serves 6

4 boneless, skinless chicken-breast halves	4–5 (1 ounce each) slices Swiss cheese
¼ cup water	¾ cup fat-free Thousand Island salad dressing
1-pound bag sauerkraut, drained and rinsed	2 tablespoons chopped fresh parsley

1. Place chicken and water in inner pot of the Instant Pot along with ¼ cup water. Layer sauerkraut over chicken. Add cheese. Top with salad dressing. Sprinkle with parsley. 2. Secure the lid and cook on the Slow Cook setting on low 6–8 hours.

Per Serving

Calorie: 217 | fat: 5g | protein: 28g | carbs: 13 | sugars: 6g | fiber: 2g | sodium: 693 mg

Speedy Chicken Cacciatore

Prep time: 5 minutes | Cook time: 30 minutes | Serves 6

2 pounds boneless, skinless chicken thighs	½ cup dry red wine
1½ teaspoons fine sea salt	1½ teaspoons Italian seasoning
½ teaspoon freshly ground black pepper	½ teaspoon red pepper flakes (optional)
2 tablespoons extra-virgin olive oil	One 14½-ounce can diced tomatoes and their liquid
3 garlic cloves, chopped	2 tablespoons tomato paste
2 large red bell peppers, seeded and cut into ¼ by 2-inch strips	Cooked brown rice or whole-grain pasta for serving
2 large yellow onions, sliced	

1. Season the chicken thighs on both sides with 1 teaspoon of the salt and the black pepper. 2. Select the Sauté setting on the Instant Pot and heat the oil and

garlic for 2 minutes, until the garlic is bubbling but not browned. Add the bell peppers, onions, and remaining ½ teaspoon salt and sauté for 3 minutes, until the onions begin to soften. Stir in the wine, Italian seasoning, and pepper flakes (if using). Using tongs, add the chicken to the pot, turning each piece to coat it in the wine and spices and nestling them in a single layer in the liquid. Pour the tomatoes and their liquid on top of the chicken and dollop the tomato paste on top. Do not stir them in. 3. Secure the lid and set the Pressure Release to Sealing. Press the Cancel button to reset the cooking program, then select the Poultry, Pressure Cook, or Manual setting and set the cooking time for 12 minutes at high pressure. (The pot will take about 15 minutes to come up to pressure before the cooking program begins.) 4. When the cooking program ends, perform a quick pressure release by moving the Pressure Release to Venting, or let the pressure release naturally. Open the pot and, using tongs, transfer the chicken and vegetables to a serving dish. 5. Spoon some of the sauce over the chicken and serve hot, with the rice on the side.

Per Serving

calories: 297 | fat: 11g | protein: 32g | carbs: 16g | sugars: 3g | fiber: 3g | sodium: 772mg

Chicken Casablanca

Prep time: 20 minutes | Cook time: 12 minutes | Serves 8

2 large onions, sliced	½ teaspoon salt
1 teaspoon ground ginger	½ teaspoon pepper
3 garlic cloves, minced	¼ teaspoon cinnamon
2 tablespoons canola oil, divided	2 tablespoons raisins
3 pounds skinless chicken pieces	14½-ounce can chopped tomatoes
3 large carrots, diced	3 small zucchini, sliced
2 large potatoes, unpeeled, diced	15-ounce can garbanzo beans, drained
½ teaspoon ground cumin	2 tablespoons chopped parsley

1. Using the Sauté function of the Instant Pot, cook the onions, ginger, and garlic in 1 tablespoon of the oil for 5 minutes, stirring constantly. Remove onions, ginger, and garlic from pot and set aside. 2. Brown the chicken pieces with the remaining oil, then add the cooked onions, ginger and garlic back in as well as all of the remaining ingredients, except the parsley. 3. Secure the lid and make sure vent is in the sealing position. Cook on Manual mode for 12 minutes. 4. When

cook time is up, let the pressure release naturally for 5 minutes and then release the rest of the pressure manually.

Per Serving

calories: 395 | fat: 10g | protein: 36g | carbs: 40g | sugars: 10g | fiber: 8g | sodium: 390mg

Thai Yellow Curry with Chicken Meatballs

Prep time: 5 minutes | Cook time: 30 minutes | Serves 4

1 pound 95 percent lean ground chicken

⅓ cup gluten-free panko (Japanese bread crumbs)

1 egg white

1 tablespoon coconut oil

1 yellow onion, cut into 1-inch pieces

One 14-ounce can light coconut milk

3 tablespoons yellow curry paste

¾ cup water

8 ounces carrots, halved lengthwise, then cut crosswise into 1-inch lengths (or quartered if very large)

8 ounces zucchini, quartered lengthwise, then cut crosswise into 1-inch lengths (or cut into halves, then thirds if large)

8 ounces cremini mushrooms, quartered

Fresh Thai basil leaves for serving (optional)

Fresno or jalapeño chile, thinly sliced, for serving (optional)

1 lime, cut into wedges

Cooked cauliflower "rice" for serving

1. In a medium bowl, combine the chicken, panko, and egg white and mix until evenly combined. Set aside. 2. Select the Sauté setting on the Instant Pot and heat the oil for 2 minutes. Add the onion and sauté for 5 minutes, until it begins to soften and brown. Add ½ cup of the coconut milk and the curry paste and sauté for 1 minute more, until bubbling and fragrant. Press the Cancel button to turn off the pot, then stir in the water. 3. Using a 1½-tablespoon cookie scoop, shape and drop meatballs into the pot in a single layer. 4. Secure the lid and set the Pressure Release to Sealing. Select the Pressure Cook or Manual setting and set the cooking time for 5 minutes at high pressure. (The pot will take about 5 minutes to come up to pressure before the cooking program begins.) 5. When the cooking program ends, perform a quick pressure release by moving the Pressure Release to Venting, or let the pressure release naturally. Open the pot and stir in the carrots, zucchini, mushrooms, and remaining 1¼ cups coconut milk. 6. Press the Cancel button to reset the cooking program, then select the Sauté setting.

Bring the curry to a simmer (this will take about 2 minutes), then let cook, uncovered, for about 8 minutes, until the carrots are fork-tender. Press the Cancel button to turn off the pot. 7. Ladle the curry into bowls. Serve piping hot, topped with basil leaves and chile slices, if desired, and the lime wedges and cauliflower "rice" on the side.

Per Serving

calories: 349 | fat: 15g | protein: 30g | carbs: 34g | sugars: 8g | fiber: 5g | sodium: 529mg

Mexican Turkey Tenderloin

Prep time: 5 minutes | Cook time: 8 minutes | Serves 6

1 cup Low-Sodium Salsa or bottled salsa	tenderloin or boneless turkey breast, cut into 6 pieces
1 teaspoon chili powder	Freshly ground black pepper
½ teaspoon ground cumin	½ cup shredded Monterey Jack cheese or Mexican cheese blend
¼ teaspoon dried oregano	
1½ pounds unseasoned turkey	

1. In a small bowl or measuring cup, combine the salsa, chili powder, cumin, and oregano. Pour half of the mixture into the electric pressure cooker. 2. Nestle the turkey into the sauce. Grind some pepper onto each piece of turkey. Pour the remaining salsa mixture on top. 3. Close and lock the lid of the pressure cooker. Set the valve to sealing. 4. Cook on high pressure for 8 minutes. 5. When the cooking is complete, hit Cancel. Allow the pressure to release naturally for 10 minutes, then quick release any remaining pressure. 6. Once the pin drops, unlock and remove the lid. 7. Sprinkle the cheese on top, and put the lid back on for a few minutes to let the cheese melt. Serve immediately.

Ground Turkey Tetrazzini

Prep time: 5 minutes | Cook time: 20 minutes | Serves 6

1 tablespoon extra-virgin olive oil

2 garlic cloves, minced

1 yellow onion, diced

8 ounces cremini or button mushrooms, sliced

½ teaspoon fine sea salt

¼ teaspoon freshly ground black pepper

1 pound 93 percent lean ground turkey

1 teaspoon poultry seasoning

6 ounces whole-grain extra-broad egg-white pasta (such as No Yolks brand) or whole-wheat elbow pasta

2 cups low-sodium chicken broth

1½ cups frozen green peas, thawed

3 cups baby spinach

Three ¾-ounce wedges Laughing Cow creamy light Swiss cheese, or 2 tablespoons Neufchâtel cheese, at room temperature

⅓ cup grated Parmesan cheese

1 tablespoon chopped fresh flat-leaf parsley

1. Select the Sauté setting on the Instant Pot and heat the oil and garlic for 2 minutes, until the garlic is bubbling but not browned. Add the onion, mushrooms, salt, and pepper and sauté for about 5 minutes, until the mushrooms have wilted and begun to give up their liquid. Add the turkey and poultry seasoning and sauté, using a wooden spoon or spatula to break up the meat as it cooks, for about 4 minutes more, until cooked through and no streaks of pink remain. 2. Stir in the pasta. Pour in the broth and use the spoon or spatula to nudge the pasta into the liquid as much as possible. It's fine if some pieces are not completely submerged. 3. Secure the lid and set the Pressure Release to Sealing. Press the Cancel button to reset the cooking program, then select the Pressure Cook or Manual setting and set the cooking time for 5 minutes at high pressure. (The pot will take about 5 minutes to come up to pressure before the cooking program begins.) 4. When the cooking program ends, let the pressure release naturally for 5 minutes, then move the Pressure Release to Venting to release any remaining steam. Open the pot and stir in the peas, spinach, Laughing Cow cheese, and Parmesan. Let stand for 2 minutes, then stir the mixture once more. 5. Ladle into bowls or onto plates and sprinkle with the parsley. Serve right away.

Per Serving

calories: 321 | fat: 11g | protein: 26g | carbs: 35g | sugars: 4g | fiber: 5g | sodium: 488mg

Greek Chicken

Prep time: 25 minutes | Cook time: 20 minutes | Serves 6

4 potatoes, unpeeled, quartered	3 teaspoons dried oregano
2 pounds chicken pieces, trimmed of skin and fat	¾ teaspoons salt
	½ teaspoons pepper
2 large onions, quartered	1 tablespoon olive oil
1 whole bulb garlic, cloves minced	1 cup water

1. Place potatoes, chicken, onions, and garlic into the inner pot of the Instant Pot, then sprinkle with seasonings. Top with oil and water. 2. Secure the lid and make sure vent is set to sealing. Cook on Manual mode for 20 minutes. 3. When cook time is over, let the pressure release naturally for 5 minutes, then release the rest manually.

Per Serving

Calorie: 278 | fat: 6g | protein: 27g | carbs: 29g | sugars: 9g | fiber: 4g | sodium: 358mg

Hard-boiled Eggs

Prep time: 2 minutes | Cook time: 2 minutes | Serves 9

9 large eggs

1. Pour 1 cup of water into the electric pressure cooker and insert an egg rack. Gently stand the eggs in the rack, fat ends down. If you don't have an egg rack, place the eggs in a steamer basket or on a wire rack. 2. Close and lock the lid of the pressure cooker. Set the valve to sealing. 3. Cook on high pressure for 2 minutes. 4. When the cooking is complete, hit Cancel and allow the pressure to release naturally. 5. Once the pin drops, unlock and remove the lid. 6. Using tongs, carefully remove the eggs from the pressure cooker. Peel or refrigerate the eggs when they are cool enough to handle.

Per Serving

calories: 78 | fat: 5g | protein: 6g | carbs: 1g | sugars: 1g | fiber: 0g | sodium: 62mg

Cheesy Stuffed Cabbage

Prep time: 30 minutes | Cook time: 18 minutes | Serves 6 to 8

1–2 heads savoy cabbage

1 pound ground turkey

1 egg

1 cup reduced-fat shredded cheddar cheese

2 tablespoons evaporated skim milk

¼ cup reduced-fat shredded Parmesan cheese

¼ cup reduced-fat shredded mozzarella cheese

¼ cup finely diced onion

¼ cup finely diced bell pepper

¼ cup finely diced mushrooms

1 teaspoon salt

½ teaspoon black pepper

1 teaspoon garlic powder

6 basil leaves, fresh and cut chiffonade

1 tablespoon fresh parsley, chopped

1 quart of your favorite pasta sauce

1. Remove the core from the cabbages. 2. Boil pot of water and place 1 head at a time into the water for approximately 10 minutes. 3. Allow cabbage to cool slightly. Once cooled, remove the leaves carefully and set aside. You'll need about 15 or 16. 4. Mix together the meat and all remaining ingredients except the pasta sauce. 5. One leaf at a time, put a heaping tablespoon of meat mixture in the center. 6. Tuck the sides in and then roll tightly. 7. Add ½ cup sauce to the bottom of the inner pot of the Instant Pot. 8. Place the rolls, fold-side down, into the pot and layer them, putting a touch of sauce between each layer and finally on top. (You may want to cook the rolls in two batches.) 9. Lock lid and make sure vent is at sealing. Set timer on 18 minutes on Manual at high pressure, then manually release the pressure when cook time is over.

Per Serving

calories: 199 | fat: 8 g | protein: 20g | carbs: 14g | sugars: 7g | fiber: 0g | sodium: 678 mg

Chapter 6 Beef, Pork, and Lamb

Shepherd's Pie with Cauliflower-Carrot Mash

Prep time: 10 minutes | Cook time: 35 minutes | Serves 6

1 tablespoon coconut oil

2 garlic cloves, minced

1 large yellow onion, diced

1 pound ground lamb

1 pound 95 percent lean ground beef

½ cup low-sodium vegetable broth

1 teaspoons dried thyme

1 teaspoon dried sage

1 teaspoon freshly ground black pepper

1¾ teaspoons fine sea salt

2 tablespoons Worcestershire sauce

One 12-ounce bag frozen baby lima beans, green peas, or shelled edamame

3 tablespoons tomato paste

1 pound cauliflower florets

1 pound carrots, halved lengthwise and then crosswise (or quartered if very large)

¼ cup coconut milk or other nondairy milk

½ cup sliced green onions, white and green parts

1. Select the Sauté setting on the Instant Pot and heat the oil and garlic for 2 minutes, until the garlic is bubbling but not browned. Add the onion and sauté for 3 minutes, until it begins to soften. Add the lamb and beef and sauté, using a wooden spoon or spatula to break up the meat as it cooks, for 6 minutes, until cooked through and no streaks of pink remain. 2. Stir in the broth, using the spoon or spatula to nudge any browned bits from the bottom of the pot. Add the thyme, sage, pepper, ¾ teaspoon of the salt, the Worcestershire sauce, and lima beans and stir to mix. Dollop the tomato paste on top. Do not stir it in. 3. Place a tall steam rack in the pot, then place the cauliflower and carrots on top of the rack. 4. Secure the lid and set the Pressure Release to Sealing. Press the Cancel button to reset the cooking program, then select the Pressure Cook or Manual setting and set the cooking time for 4 minutes at low pressure. (The pot will take about 15 minutes to come up to pressure before the cooking program begins.) 5. Position an oven rack 4 to 6 inches below the heat source and preheat the broiler. 6. When the cooking program ends, perform a quick pressure release by moving the Pressure Release to Venting. Open the pot and, using tongs, transfer the cauliflower and carrots to a bowl. Add the coconut milk and remaining 1 teaspoon salt to the bowl. Using an immersion blender, blend the vegetables until smooth.

7. Wearing heat-resistant mitts, remove the steam rack from the pot. Stir ½ cup of the mashed vegetables into the filling mixture in the pot, incorporating the tomato paste at the same time. Remove the inner pot from the housing. Transfer the mixture to a broiler-safe 9 by 13-inch baking dish, spreading it in an even layer. Dollop the mashed vegetables on top and spread them out evenly with a fork. Broil, checking often, for 5 to 8 minutes, until the mashed vegetables are lightly browned. 8. Spoon the shepherd's pie onto plates, sprinkle with the green onions, and serve hot.

Per Serving

calories: 437 | fat: 18g | protein: 39g | carbs: 33g | sugars: 8g | fiber: 9g | sodium: 802mg

Pot Roast with Gravy and Vegetables

Prep time: 30 minutes | Cook time: 1 hour 15 minutes | Serves 6

1 tablespoon olive oil	1 teaspoon Kitchen Bouquet, or gravy browning seasoning sauce
3–4 pound bottom round, rump, or arm roast, trimmed of fat	1 garlic clove, minced
¼ teaspoon salt	2 medium onions, cut in wedges
2–3 teaspoons pepper	4 medium potatoes, cubed, unpeeled
2 tablespoons flour	2 carrots, quartered
1 cup cold water	1 green bell pepper, sliced

1. Press the Sauté button on the Instant Pot and pour the oil inside, letting it heat up. Sprinkle each side of the roast with salt and pepper, then brown it for 5 minutes on each side inside the pot. 2. Mix together the flour, water and Kitchen Bouquet and spread over roast. 3. Add garlic, onions, potatoes, carrots, and green pepper. 4. Secure the lid and make sure the vent is set to sealing. Press Manual and set the Instant Pot for 1 hour and 15 minutes. 5. When cook time is up, let the pressure release naturally.

Per Serving

calories: 551 | fat: 30g | protein: 49g | carbs: 19g | sugars: 2g | fiber: 3g | sodium: 256mg

Beef Burgundy

Prep time: 30 minutes | Cook time: 30 minutes | Serves 6

2 tablespoons olive oil	1 teaspoon salt
2 pounds stewing meat, cubed, trimmed of fat	¼ teaspoon dried marjoram
	¼ teaspoon dried thyme
2½ tablespoons flour	⅛ teaspoon pepper
5 medium onions, thinly sliced	¾ cup beef broth
½ pound fresh mushrooms, sliced	1½ cups burgundy

1. Press Sauté on the Instant pot and add in the olive oil. 2. Dredge meat in flour, then brown in batches in the Instant Pot. Set aside the meat. Sauté the onions and mushrooms in the remaining oil and drippings for about 3–4 minutes, then add the meat back in. Press Cancel. 3. Add the salt, marjoram, thyme, pepper, broth, and wine to the Instant Pot. 4. Secure the lid and make sure the vent is set to sealing. Press the Manual button and set to 30 minutes. 5. When cook time is up, let the pressure release naturally for 15 minutes, then perform a quick release. 6. Serve over cooked noodles.

Per Serving

calories: 358 | fat: 11g | protein: 37g | carbs: 15g | sugars: 5g | fiber: 2g | sodium: 472mg

Mexican Lasagna

Prep time: 15 minutes | Cook time: 15 minutes | Serves 4

Nonstick cooking spray
½ (15-ounce) can light red kidney beans, rinsed and drained
4 (6-inch) gluten-free corn tortillas
1½ cups cooked shredded beef, pork, or chicken
1⅓ cups salsa
1⅓ cups shredded Mexican cheese blend

1. Spray a 6-inch springform pan with nonstick spray. Wrap the bottom in foil. 2. In a medium bowl, mash the beans with a fork. 3. Place 1 tortilla in the bottom of the pan. Add about ⅓ of the beans, ½ cup of meat, ⅓ cup of salsa, and ⅓ cup of cheese. Press down. Repeat for 2 more layers. Add the remaining tortilla

and press down. Top with the remaining salsa and cheese. There are no beans or meat on the top layer. 4. Tear off a piece of foil big enough to cover the pan, and spray it with nonstick spray. Line the pan with the foil, sprayed-side down. 5. Pour 1 cup of water into the electric pressure cooker. 6. Place the pan on the wire rack and carefully lower it into the pot. Close and lock the lid of the pressure cooker. Set the valve to sealing. 7. Cook on high pressure for 15 minutes. 8. When the cooking is complete, hit Cancel. Allow the pressure to release naturally for 10 minutes, then quick release any remaining pressure. 9. Once the pin drops, unlock and remove the lid. 10. Using the handles of the wire rack, carefully remove the pan from the pot. Let the lasagna sit for 5 minutes. Carefully remove the ring. 11. Slice into quarters and serve.

49. BBQ Ribs and Broccoli Slaw

Prep time: 10 minutes | Cook time: 50 minutes | Serves 6

BBQ Ribs	pepper
4 pounds baby back ribs	1 pound broccoli florets (or florets
1 teaspoon fine sea salt	from 2 large crowns), chopped
1 teaspoon freshly ground black	10 radishes, halved and thinly sliced
pepper	1 red bell pepper, seeded and cut
Broccoli Slaw	lengthwise into narrow strips
½ cup plain 2 percent Greek yogurt	1 large apple (such as Fuji, Jonagold,
1 tablespoon olive oil	or Gala), thinly sliced
1 tablespoon fresh lemon juice	½ red onion, thinly sliced
½ teaspoon fine sea salt	¾ cup low-sugar or unsweetened
¼ teaspoon freshly ground black	barbecue sauce

1. To make the ribs: Pat the ribs dry with paper towels, then cut the racks into six sections (three to five ribs per section, depending on how big the racks are). Season the ribs all over with the salt and pepper. 2. Pour 1 cup water into the Instant Pot and place the wire metal steam rack into the pot. Place the ribs on top of the wire rack (it's fine to stack them up). 3. Secure the lid and set the Pressure Release to Sealing. Select the Pressure Cook or Manual setting and set the cooking time for 20 minutes at high pressure. (The pot will take about 15 minutes to come up to pressure before the cooking program begins.) 4. To make the broccoli slaw: While the ribs are cooking, in a small bowl, stir together the yogurt, oil, lemon juice, salt, and pepper, mixing well. In a large bowl, combine the

broccoli, radishes, bell pepper, apple, and onion. Drizzle with the yogurt mixture and toss until evenly coated. 5. When the ribs have about 10 minutes left in their cooking time, preheat the oven to 400°F. Line a sheet pan with aluminum foil. 6. When the cooking program ends, perform a quick pressure release by moving the Pressure Release to Venting. Open the pot and, using tongs, transfer the ribs in a single layer to the prepared sheet pan. Brush the barbecue sauce onto both sides of the ribs, using 2 tablespoons of sauce per section of ribs. Bake, meaty-side up, for 15 to 20 minutes, until lightly browned. 7. Serve the ribs warm, with the slaw on the side.

Per Serving

calories: 392 | fat: 15g | protein: 45g | carbs: 19g | sugars: 9g | fiber: 4g | sodium: 961mg

50. Zesty Swiss Steak

Prep time: 35 minutes | Cook time: 35 minutes | Serves 6

3–4 tablespoons flour	1 cup sliced onions
½ teaspoon salt	1 pound carrots, sliced
¼ teaspoon pepper	14½-ounce can whole tomatoes
1½ teaspoons dry mustard	⅓ cup water
1½–2 pounds round steak, trimmed of fat	1 tablespoon brown sugar
	1½ tablespoons Worcestershire sauce
1 tablespoon canola oil	

1. Combine flour, salt, pepper, and dry mustard. 2. Cut steak in serving pieces. Dredge in flour mixture. 3. Set the Instant Pot to Sauté and add in the oil. Brown the steak pieces on both sides in the oil. Press Cancel. 4. Add onions and carrots into the Instant Pot. 5. Combine the tomatoes, water, brown sugar, and Worcestershire sauce. Pour into the Instant Pot. 6. Secure the lid and make sure the vent is set to sealing. Press Manual and set the time for 35 minutes. 7. When cook time is up, let the pressure release naturally for 15 minutes, then perform a quick release.

Per Serving

calories: 236 | fat: 8g | protein:23g | carbs: 18g | sugars: 9g | fiber: 3g | sodium: 9g

Pork Butt Roast

Prep time: 10 minutes | Cook time: 9 minutes | Serves 6 to 8

3–4-pound pork butt roast
2–3 tablespoons of your favorite rub
2 cups water

1. Place pork in the inner pot of the Instant Pot. 2. Sprinkle in the rub all over the roast and add the water, being careful not to wash off the rub. 3. Secure the lid and set the vent to sealing. Cook for 9 minutes on the Manual setting. 4. Let the pressure release naturally.

Per Serving

calories: 598 | fat: 40g | protein: 57g | carbs: 0g | sugars: 0g | fiber: 0g | sodium: 152mg

Quick Steak Tacos

Prep time: 5 minutes | Cook time: 10 minutes | Serves 6

1 tablespoon olive oil
8 ounces sirloin steak
2 tablespoons steak seasoning
1 teaspoon Worcestershire sauce
½ red onion, halved and sliced
6 corn tortillas
¼ cup tomatoes
¾ cup reduced-fat Mexican cheese
2 tablespoons low-fat sour cream
6 tablespoons garden fresh salsa
¼ cup chopped fresh cilantro

1. Turn the Instant Pot on the Sauté function. When the pot displays "hot," add the olive oil to the pot. 2. Season the steak with the steak seasoning. 3. Add the steak to the pot along with the Worcestershire sauce. 4. Cook each side of the steak for 2–3 minutes until the steak turns brown. 5. Remove the steak from the pot and slice thinly. 6. Add the onion to the pot with the remaining olive oil and steak juices and cook them until translucent. 7. Remove the onion from the pot. 8. Warm your corn tortillas, then assemble your steak, onion, tomatoes, cheese, sour cream, salsa, and cilantro on top of each.

Per Serving

calories: 187 | fat: 9g | protein: 14g | carbs: 14g | sugars: 2g | fiber: 2g | sodium: 254mg

Carnitas Burrito Bowls

Prep time: 10 minutes | Cook time: 1 hour | Serves 6

Carnitas

1 tablespoon chili powder

½ teaspoon garlic powder

1 teaspoon ground coriander

1 teaspoon fine sea salt

½ cup water

¼ cup fresh lime juice

One 2-pound boneless pork shoulder butt roast, cut into 2-inch cubes

Rice and Beans

1 cup Minute brand brown rice (see Note)

1½ cups drained cooked black beans, or one 15-ounce can black beans, rinsed and drained

Pico de Gallo

8 ounces tomatoes (see Note), diced

½ small yellow onion, diced

1 jalapeño chile, seeded and finely diced

1 tablespoon chopped fresh cilantro

1 teaspoon fresh lime juice

Pinch of fine sea salt

¼ cup sliced green onions, white and green parts

2 tablespoons chopped fresh cilantro

3 hearts romaine lettuce, cut into ¼-inch-wide ribbons

2 large avocados, pitted, peeled, and sliced

Hot sauce (such as Cholula or Tapatío) for serving

1. To make the carnitas: In a small bowl, combine the chili powder, garlic powder, coriander, and salt and mix well. 2. Pour the water and lime juice into the Instant Pot. Add the pork, arranging the pieces in a single layer. Sprinkle the chili powder mixture evenly over the pork. 3. Secure the lid and set the Pressure Release to Sealing. Select the Meat/Stew setting and set the cooking time for 30 minutes at high pressure. (The pot will take about 10 minutes to come up to pressure before the cooking program begins.) 4. When the cooking program ends, let the pressure release naturally for at least 15 minutes, then move the Pressure Release to Venting to release any remaining steam. Open the pot and, using tongs, transfer the pork to a plate or cutting board. 5. While the pressure is releasing, preheat the oven to 400°F. 6. Wearing heat-resistant mitts, lift out the inner pot and pour the cooking liquid into a fat separator. Pour the defatted cooking liquid into a liquid measuring cup and discard the fat. (Alternatively, use a ladle or large spoon to skim the fat off the surface of the liquid.) Add water as needed to the cooking liquid to total 1 cup (you may have enough without adding water). 7. To make the rice and beans: Pour the 1 cup cooking liquid into the Instant Pot and add the rice,

making sure it is in an even layer. Place a tall steam rack into the pot. Add the black beans to a 1½-quart stainless-steel bowl and place the bowl on top of the rack. (The bowl should not touch the lid once the pot is closed.) 8. Secure the lid and set the Pressure Release to Sealing. Press the Cancel button to reset the cooking program, then select the Pressure Cook or Manual setting and set the cooking time for 15 minutes at high pressure. (The pot will take about 5 minutes to come to pressure before the cooking program begins.) 9. While the rice and beans are cooking, using two forks, shred the meat into bite-size pieces. Transfer the pork to a sheet pan, spreading it out in an even layer. Place in the oven for 20 minutes, until crispy and browned. 10. To make the pico de gallo: While the carnitas, rice, and beans are cooking, in a medium bowl, combine the tomatoes, onion, jalapeño, cilantro, lime juice, and salt and mix well. Set aside. 11. When the cooking program ends, let the pressure release naturally for 5 minutes, then move the Pressure Release to Venting to release any remaining steam. Open the pot and, wearing heat-resistant mitts, remove the bowl of beans and then the steam rack from the pot. Then remove the inner pot. Add the green onions and cilantro to the rice and, using a fork, fluff the rice and mix in the green onions and cilantro. 12. Divide the rice, beans, carnitas, pico de gallo, lettuce, and avocados evenly among six bowls. Serve warm, with the hot sauce on the side.

Per Serving

calories: 447 | fat: 20g | protein: 31g | carbs: 35g | sugars: 4g | fiber: 9g | sodium: 653mg

Pork Carnitas

Prep time: 10 minutes | Cook time: 20 minutes | Serves 8

1 teaspoon kosher salt	Juice and zest of 1 large orange
2 teaspoons chili powder	Juice and zest of 1 medium lime
2 teaspoons dried oregano	6-inch gluten-free corn tortillas,
½ teaspoon freshly ground black	warmed, for serving (optional)
pepper	Chopped avocado, for serving
1 (2½-pound) pork sirloin roast or	(optional)
boneless pork butt, cut into 1½-inch	Roasted Tomatillo Salsa or salsa verde,
cubes	for serving (optional)
2 tablespoons avocado oil, divided	Shredded cheddar cheese, for serving
3 garlic cloves, minced	(optional)

1. In a large bowl or gallon-size zip-top bag, combine the salt, chili powder, oregano, and pepper. Add the pork cubes and toss to coat. 2. Set the electric pressure cooker to the Sauté/More setting. When the pot is hot, pour in 1 tablespoon of avocado oil. 3. Add half of the pork to the pot and sear until the pork is browned on all sides, about 5 minutes. Transfer the pork to a plate, add the remaining 1 tablespoon of avocado oil to the pot, and sear the remaining pork. Hit Cancel. 4. Return all of the pork to the pot and add the garlic, orange zest and juice, and lime zest and juice to the pot. 5. Close and lock the lid of the pressure cooker. Set the valve to sealing. 6. Cook on high pressure for 20 minutes. 7. When the cooking is complete, hit Cancel. Allow the pressure to release naturally for 15 minutes then quick release any remaining pressure. 8. Once the pin drops, unlock and remove the lid. 9. Using two forks, shred the meat right in the pot. 10. (Optional) For more authentic carnitas, spread the shredded meat on a broiler-safe sheet pan. Preheat the broiler with the rack 6 inches from the heating element. Broil the pork for about 5 minutes or until it begins to crisp. (Watch carefully so you don't let the pork burn.) 11. Place the pork in a serving bowl. Top with some of the juices from the pot. Serve with tortillas, avocado, salsa, and Cheddar cheese (if using).

Mary's Sunday Pot Roast

Prep time: 10 minutes | Cook time:1 hour 30 minutes | Serves 10

1 (3- to 4-pound) beef rump roast	1 tablespoon minced garlic
2 teaspoons kosher salt, divided	3 cups low-sodium beef broth
2 tablespoons avocado oil	1 teaspoon freshly ground black
1 large onion, coarsely chopped (about	pepper
1½ cups)	1 tablespoon dried parsley
4 large carrots, each cut into 4 pieces	2 tablespoons all-purpose flour

1. Rub the roast all over with 1 teaspoon of the salt. 2. Set the electric pressure cooker to the Sauté setting. When the pot is hot, pour in the avocado oil. 3. Carefully place the roast in the pot and sear it for 6 to 9 minutes on each side. (You want a dark caramelized crust.) Hit Cancel. 4. Transfer the roast from the pot to a plate. 5. In order, put the onion, carrots, and garlic in the pot. Place the roast on top of the vegetables along with any juices that accumulated on the plate. 6. In a medium bowl, whisk together the broth, remaining 1 teaspoon of salt, pepper, and parsley. Pour the broth mixture over the roast. 7. Close and lock the

lid of the pressure cooker. Set the valve to sealing. 8. Cook on high pressure for 1 hour and 30 minutes. 9. When the cooking is complete, hit Cancel and allow the pressure to release naturally. 10. Once the pin drops, unlock and remove the lid. 11. Using large slotted spoons, transfer the roast and vegetables to a serving platter while you make the gravy. 12. Using a large spoon or fat separator, remove the fat from the juices in the pot. Set the electric pressure cooker to the Sauté setting and bring the liquid to a boil. 13. In a small bowl, whisk together the flour and 4 tablespoons of water to make a slurry. Pour the slurry into the pot, whisking occasionally, until the gravy is the thickness you like. Season with salt and pepper, if necessary. 14. Serve the meat and carrots with the gravy.

Per Serving

calories: 245 | fat: 10g | protein: 33g | carbs: 6g | sugars: 2g | fiber: 1g | sodium: 397mg

Spicy Beef Stew with Butternut Squash

Prep time: 15 minutes | Cook time: 30 minutes | Serves 8

1½ tablespoons smoked paprika	1 cup low-sodium beef or vegetable broth
2 teaspoons ground cinnamon	
1½ teaspoons kosher salt	1 medium red onion, cut into wedges
1 teaspoon ground ginger	8 garlic cloves, minced
1 teaspoon red pepper flakes	1 (28-ounce) carton or can no-salt-added diced tomatoes
½ teaspoon freshly ground black pepper	
	2 pounds butternut squash, peeled and cut into 1-inch pieces
2 pounds beef shoulder roast, cut into 1-inch cubes	
	Chopped fresh cilantro or parsley, for serving
2 tablespoons avocado oil, divided	

1. In a zip-top bag or medium bowl, combine the paprika, cinnamon, salt, ginger, red pepper, and black pepper. Add the beef and toss to coat. 2. Set the electric pressure cooker to the Sauté setting. When the pot is hot, pour in 1 tablespoon of avocado oil. 3. Add half of the beef to the pot and cook, stirring occasionally, for 3 to 5 minutes or until the beef is no longer pink. Transfer it to a plate, then add the remaining 1 tablespoon of avocado oil and brown the remaining beef. Transfer to the plate. Hit Cancel. 4. Stir in the broth and scrape up any brown bits from the bottom of the pot. Return the beef to the pot and add the onion, garlic, tomatoes and their juices, and squash. Stir well. 5. Close and lock lid of pressure cooker. Set

the valve to sealing. 6. Cook on high pressure for 30 minutes. 7. When cooking is complete, hit Cancel. Allow the pressure to release naturally for 10 minutes, then quick release any remaining pressure. 8. Unlock and remove lid. Spoon into serving bowls, sprinkle with cilantro or parsley, and serve.

Bavarian Beef

Prep time: 35 minutes | Cook time: 1 hour 15 minutes | Serves 8

1 tablespoon canola oil	⅓ cup German-style mustard
3-pound boneless beef chuck roast, trimmed of fat	2 teaspoons coarsely ground black pepper
3 cups sliced carrots	2 bay leaves
3 cups sliced onions	¼ teaspoon ground cloves
2 large kosher dill pickles, chopped	1 cup water
1 cup sliced celery	⅓ cup flour
½ cup dry red wine or beef broth	

1. Press Sauté on the Instant Pot and add in the oil. Brown roast on both sides for about 5 minutes. Press Cancel. 2. Add all of the remaining ingredients, except for the flour, to the Instant Pot. 3. Secure the lid and make sure the vent is set to sealing. Press Manual and set the time to 1 hour and 15 minutes. Let the pressure release naturally. 4. Remove meat and vegetables to large platter. Cover to keep warm. 5. Remove 1 cup of the liquid from the Instant Pot and mix with the flour. Press Sauté on the Instant Pot and add the flour/broth mixture back in, whisking. Cook until the broth is smooth and thickened. 6. Serve over noodles or spaetzle.

Per Serving
Calorie: 251 | fat: 8g | protein: 26g | carbs: 17g | sugars: 7g | fiber: 4g | sodium: 525 mg

Easy Pot Roast and Vegetables

Prep time: 20 minutes | Cook time: 35 minutes | Serves 6

3–4 pound chuck roast, trimmed of fat and cut into serving-sized chunks	baby carrots
4 medium potatoes, cubed, unpeeled	2 celery ribs, sliced thin
4 medium carrots, sliced, or 1 pound	1 envelope dry onion soup mix
	3 cups water

1. Place the pot roast chunks and vegetables into the Instant Pot along with the potatoes, carrots and celery. 2. Mix together the onion soup mix and water and pour over the contents of the Instant Pot. 3. Secure the lid and make sure the vent is set to sealing. Set the Instant Pot to Manual mode for 35 minutes. Let pressure release naturally when cook time is up.

Per Serving

Calorie: 325 | fat: 8g | protein: 35g | carbs: 26g | sugars: 6g | fiber: 4g | sodium: 560mg

Garlic Beef Stroganoff

Prep time: 20 minutes | Cook time: 25 minutes | Serves 6

2 tablespoons canola oil	10¾-ounce can 98% fat-free,
1½ pounds boneless round steak, cut into thin strips, trimmed of fat	lower-sodium cream of mushroom soup
2 teaspoons sodium-free beef bouillon powder	1 large onion, chopped
	3 garlic cloves, minced
1 cup mushroom juice, with water added to make a full cup	1 tablespoon Worcestershire sauce
2 (4½-ounce) jars sliced mushrooms, drained with juice reserved	6-ounces fat-free cream cheese, cubed and softened

1. Press the Sauté button and put the oil into the Instant Pot inner pot. 2. Once the oil is heated, sauté the beef until it is lightly browned, about 2 minutes on each side. Set the beef aside for a moment. Press Cancel and wipe out the Instant Pot with some paper towel. 3. Press Sauté again and dissolve the bouillon in the mushroom juice and water in inner pot of the Instant Pot. Once dissolved, press Cancel. 4. Add the mushrooms, soup, onion, garlic, and Worcestershire sauce and stir. Add the beef back to the pot. 5. Secure the lid and make sure the vent is set to sealing. Press Manual and set for 15 minutes. 6. When cook time is up, let the pressure release naturally for 15 minutes, then perform a quick release. 7. Press Cancel and remove the lid. Press Sauté. Stir in cream cheese until smooth. 8. Serve over noodles.

Per Serving

calories: 202 | fat: 8g | protein: 21g | carbs: 10g | sugars: 4g | fiber: 2g | sodium: 474mg

Chapter 6 Fish and Seafood

Lemon Pepper Tilapia with Broccoli and Carrots

Prep time: 10 minutes | Cook time: 15 minutes | Serves 4

1 pound tilapia fillets	½ cup low-sodium vegetable broth
1 teaspoon lemon pepper seasoning	2 tablespoons fresh lemon juice
¼ teaspoon fine sea salt	1 pound broccoli crowns, cut into
2 tablespoons extra-virgin olive oil	bite-size florets
2 garlic cloves, minced	8 ounces carrots, cut into ¼-inch
1 small yellow onion, sliced	thick rounds

1. Sprinkle the tilapia fillets all over with the lemon pepper seasoning and salt. 2. Select the Sauté setting on the Instant Pot and heat the oil and garlic for 2 minutes, until the garlic is bubbling but not browned. Add the onion and sauté for about 3 minutes more, until it begins to soften. 3. Pour in the broth and lemon juice, then use a wooden spoon to nudge any browned bits from the bottom of the pot. Using tongs, add the fish fillets to the pot in a single layer; it's fine if they overlap slightly. Place the broccoli and carrots on top. 4. Secure the lid and set the Pressure Release to Sealing. Press the Cancel button to reset the cooking program, then select the Pressure Cook or Manual setting and set the cooking time for 1 minute at low pressure. (The pot will take about 10 minutes to come up to pressure before the cooking program begins.) 5. When the cooking program ends, let the pressure release naturally for 10 minutes (don't open the pot before the 10 minutes are up, even if the float valve has gone down), then move the Pressure Release to Venting to release any remaining steam. Open the pot. Use a fish spatula to transfer the vegetables and fillets to plates. Serve right away.

Per Serving

calories: 243 | fat: 9g | protein: 28g | carbs: 15g | sugars: 4g | fiber: 5g | sodium: 348mg

Salade Niçoise with Oil-Packed Tuna

Prep time: 5 minutes | Cook time: 20 minutes | Serves 4

8 ounces small red potatoes, quartered
8 ounces green beans, trimmed
4 large eggs
FRENCH Vinaigrette
2 tablespoons extra-virgin olive oil
2 tablespoons cold-pressed avocado oil
2 tablespoons white wine vinegar
1 tablespoon water
1 teaspoon Dijon mustard
½ teaspoon dried oregano
¼ teaspoon fine sea salt

1 tablespoon minced shallot
2 hearts romaine lettuce, leaves separated and torn into bite-size pieces
½ cup grape tomatoes, halved
¼ cup pitted Niçoise or Greek olives
One 7-ounce can oil-packed tuna, drained and flaked
Freshly ground black pepper
1 tablespoon chopped fresh flat-leaf parsley

1. Pour 1 cup water into the Instant Pot and place a steamer basket into the pot. Add the potatoes, green beans, and eggs to the basket. 2. Secure the lid and set the Pressure Release to Sealing. Select the Steam setting and set the cooking time for 3 minutes at high pressure. (The pot will take about 15 minutes to come up to pressure before the cooking program begins.) 3. To make the vinaigrette: While the vegetables and eggs are steaming, in a small jar or other small container with a tight-fitting lid, combine the olive oil, avocado oil, vinegar, water, mustard, oregano, salt, and shallot and shake vigorously to emulsify. Set aside. 4. Prepare an ice bath. 5. When the cooking program ends, perform a quick release by moving the Pressure Release to Venting. Open the pot and, wearing heat-resistant mitts, lift out the steamer basket. Using tongs, transfer the eggs and green beans to the ice bath, leaving the potatoes in the steamer basket. 6. While the eggs and green beans are cooling, divide the lettuce, tomatoes, olives, and tuna among four shallow individual bowls. Drain the eggs and green beans. Peel and halve the eggs lengthwise, then arrange them on the salads along with the green beans and potatoes. 7. Spoon the vinaigrette over the salads and sprinkle with the pepper and parsley. Serve right away.

Per Serving

calories: 367 | fat: 23g | protein: 20g | carbs: 23g | sugars: 7g | fiber: 4g | sodium: 268mg

Shrimp Louie Salad with Thousand Island Dressing

Prep time: 5 minutes | Cook time: 20 minutes | Serves 4

2 cups water

1½ teaspoons fine sea salt

1 pound medium shrimp, peeled and deveined

4 large eggs

Thousand island Dressing

¼ cup no-sugar-added ketchup

¼ cup mayonnaise

1 tablespoon fresh lemon juice

1 teaspoon Worcestershire sauce

⅛ teaspoon cayenne pepper

Freshly ground black pepper

2 green onions, white and green parts, sliced thinly

2 hearts romaine lettuce or 1 head iceberg lettuce, shredded

1 English cucumber, sliced

8 radishes, sliced

1 cup cherry tomatoes, sliced

1 large avocado, pitted, peeled, and sliced

1. Combine the water and salt in the Instant Pot and stir to dissolve the salt. 2. Secure the lid and set the Pressure Release to Sealing. Select the Steam setting and set the cooking time for 0 (zero) minutes at low pressure. (The pot will take about 10 minutes to come up to pressure before the cooking program begins.) 3. Meanwhile, prepare an ice bath. 4. When the cooking program ends, perform a quick release by moving the Pressure Release to Venting. Open the pot and stir in the shrimp, using a wooden spoon to nudge them all down into the water. Cover the pot and leave the shrimp for 2 minutes on the Keep Warm setting. The shrimp will gently poach and cook through. Uncover the pot and, wearing heat-resistant mitts, lift out the inner pot and drain the shrimp in a colander. Transfer them to the ice bath to cool for 5 minutes, then drain them in the colander and set aside in the refrigerator. 5. Rinse out the inner pot and return it to the housing. Pour in 1 cup water and place the wire metal steam rack into the pot. Place the eggs on top of the steam rack. 6. Secure the lid and set the Pressure Release to Sealing. Press the Cancel button to reset the cooking program, then select the Egg, Pressure Cook, or Manual setting and set the cooking time for 5 minutes at high pressure. (The pot will take about 5 minutes to come up to pressure before the cooking program begins.) 7. While the eggs are cooking, prepare another ice bath. 8. When the cooking program ends, let the pressure release naturally for 5 minutes, then move the Pressure Release to Venting to release any remaining steam. Using tongs, transfer the eggs to the ice bath and let

cool for 5 minutes. 9. To make the dressing: In a small bowl, stir together the ketchup, mayonnaise, lemon juice, Worcestershire sauce, cayenne, ¼ teaspoon black pepper, and green onions. 10. Arrange the lettuce, cucumber, radishes, tomatoes, and avocado on individual plates or in large, shallow individual bowls. Mound the cooked shrimp in the center of each salad. Peel the eggs, quarter them lengthwise, and place the quarters around the shrimp. 11. Spoon the dressing over the salads and top with additional black pepper. Serve right away.

Per Serving

calories: 407 | fat: 23g | protein: 35g | carbs: 16g | sugars: 10g | fiber: 6g | sodium: 1099mg

Asian Cod with Brown Rice, Asparagus, and Mushrooms

Prep time: 5 minutes | Cook time: 25 minutes | Serves 2

¾ cup Minute brand brown rice	2 green onions, white and green parts, thinly sliced
½ cup water	
Two 5-ounce skinless cod fillets	12 ounces asparagus, trimmed
1 tablespoon soy sauce or tamari	4 ounces shiitake mushrooms, stems removed and sliced
1 tablespoon fresh lemon juice	
½ teaspoon peeled and grated fresh ginger	⅛ teaspoon fine sea salt
	⅛ teaspoon freshly ground black pepper
1 tablespoon extra-virgin olive oil or 1 tablespoon unsalted butter, cut into 8 pieces	Lemon wedges for serving

1. Pour 1 cup water into the Instant Pot. Have ready two-tier stackable stainless-steel containers. 2. In one of the containers, combine the rice and ½ cup water, then gently shake the container to spread the rice into an even layer, making sure all of the grains are submerged. Place the fish fillets on top of the rice. In a small bowl, stir together the soy sauce, lemon juice, and ginger. Pour the soy sauce mixture over the fillets. Drizzle 1 teaspoon olive oil on each fillet (or top with two pieces of the butter), and sprinkle the green onions on and around the fish. 3. In the second container, arrange the asparagus in the center in as even a layer as possible. Place the mushrooms on either side of the asparagus. Drizzle with the remaining 2 teaspoons olive oil (or put the remaining six pieces butter on top of the asparagus, spacing them evenly). Sprinkle the salt and pepper evenly over the vegetables. 4. Place the container with the rice and fish on the

bottom and the vegetable container on top. Cover the top container with its lid and then latch the containers together. Grasping the handle, lower the containers into the Instant Pot. 5. Secure the lid and set the Pressure Release to Sealing. Select the Pressure Cook or Manual setting and set the cooking time for 15 minutes at high pressure. (The pot will take about 10 minutes to come up to pressure before the cooking program begins.) 6. When the cooking program ends, let the pressure release naturally for 5 minutes, then move the Pressure Release to Venting to release any remaining steam. Open the pot and, wearing heat-resistant mitts, lift out the stacked containers. Unlatch, unstack, and open the containers, taking care not to get burned by the steam. 7. Transfer the vegetables, rice, and fish to plates and serve right away, with the lemon wedges on the side.

Per Serving

calories: 344 | fat: 11g | protein: 27g | carbs: 46g | sugars: 6g | fiber: 7g | sodium: 637mg

Mediterranean Salmon with Whole-Wheat Couscous

Prep time: 5 minutes | Cook time: 30 minutes | Serves 4

Couscous
1 cup whole-wheat couscous
1 cup water
1 tablespoon extra-virgin olive oil
1 teaspoon dried basil
¼ teaspoon fine sea salt
1 pint cherry or grape tomatoes, halved
8 ounces zucchini, halved lengthwise, then sliced crosswise ¼ inch thick
Salmon

1 pound skinless salmon fillet
2 teaspoons extra-virgin olive oil
1 tablespoon fresh lemon juice
1 garlic clove, minced
¼ teaspoon dried oregano
¼ teaspoon fine sea salt
¼ teaspoon freshly ground black pepper
1 tablespoon capers, drained
Lemon wedges for serving

1. Pour 1 cup water into the Instant Pot. Have ready two-tier stackable stainless-steel containers. 2. To make the couscous: In one of the containers, stir together the couscous, water, oil, basil, and salt. Sprinkle the tomatoes and zucchini over the top. 3. To make the salmon: Place the salmon fillet in the second container. In a small bowl, whisk together the oil, lemon juice, garlic, oregano, salt, pepper, and capers. Spoon the oil mixture over the top of the

salmon. 4. Place the container with the couscous and vegetables on the bottom and the salmon container on top. Cover the top container with its lid and then latch the containers together. Grasping the handle, lower the containers into the Instant Pot. 5. Secure the lid and set the Pressure Release to Sealing. Select the Pressure Cook or Manual setting and set the cooking time for 20 minutes at high pressure. (The pot will take about 10 minutes to come up to pressure before the cooking program begins.) 6. When the cooking program ends, let the pressure release naturally for 5 minutes, then move the Pressure Release to Venting to release any remaining steam. Open the pot and, wearing heat-resistant mitts, lift out the stacked containers. Unlatch, unstack, and open the containers, taking care not to get burned by the steam. 7. Using a fork, fluff the couscous and mix in the vegetables. Spoon the couscous onto plates, then use a spatula to cut the salmon into four pieces and place a piece on top of each couscous serving. Serve right away, with lemon wedges on the side.

Per Serving

calories: 427 | fat: 18g | protein: 28g | carbs: 36g | sugars: 2g | fiber: 6g | sodium: 404mg

Chapter 7 Stews and Soups

Butternut Squash Soup

Prep time: 30 minutes | Cook time: 15 minutes | Serves 4

2 tablespoons margarine	Salt and pepper to taste
1 large onion, chopped	2 large butternut squash, peeled,
2 cloves garlic, minced	seeded, and cubed (about 4 pounds)
1 teaspoon thyme	4 cups low-sodium chicken stock
½ teaspoon sage	

1. In the inner pot of the Instant Pot, melt the margarine using Sauté function. 2. Add onion and garlic and cook until soft, 3 to 5 minutes. 3. Add thyme and sage and cook another minute. Season with salt and pepper. 4. Stir in butternut squash and add chicken stock. 5. Secure the lid and make sure vent is at sealing. Using Manual setting, cook squash and seasonings 10 minutes, using high pressure. 6. When time is up, do a quick release of the pressure. 7. Puree the soup in a food processor or use immersion blender right in the inner pot. If soup is too

thick, add more stock. Adjust salt and pepper as needed.

Per Serving

calories: 279 | fat: 7g | protein: 6g | carbs: 56g | sugars: 10g | fiber: 9g | sodium: 144mg

Hearty Hamburger and Lentil Stew

Prep time: 15 minutes | Cook time: 55 minutes | Serves 8

2 tablespoons cold-pressed avocado oil

2 garlic cloves, chopped

1 large yellow onion, diced

2 carrots, diced

2 celery stalks, diced

2 pounds 95 percent lean ground beef

½ cup small green lentils

2 cups low-sodium roasted beef bone broth or vegetable broth

1 tablespoon Italian seasoning

1 tablespoon paprika

1½ teaspoons fine sea salt

1 extra-large russet potato, diced

1 cup frozen green peas

1 cup frozen corn

One 14½-ounce can no-salt petite diced tomatoes and their liquid

¼ cup tomato paste

1. Select the Sauté setting on the Instant Pot and heat the oil and garlic for 3 minutes, until the garlic is bubbling but not browned. Add the onion, carrots, and celery and sauté for 5 minutes, until the onion begins to soften. Add the beef and sauté, using a wooden spoon or spatula to break up the meat as it cooks, for 6 minutes, until cooked through and no streaks of pink remain. 2. Stir in the lentils, broth, Italian seasoning, paprika, and salt. Add the potato, peas, corn, and tomatoes and their liquid in layers on top of the lentils and beef, then add the tomato paste in a dollop on top. Do not stir in the vegetables and tomato paste. 3. Secure the lid and set the Pressure Release to Sealing. Press the Cancel button to reset the cooking program, then select the Pressure Cook or Manual setting and set the cooking time for 20 minutes at high pressure. (The pot will take about 20 minutes to come up to pressure before the cooking program begins.) 4. When the cooking program ends, let the pressure release naturally for at least 15 minutes, then move the Pressure Release to Venting to release any remaining steam. Open the pot and stir the stew to mix all of the ingredients. 5. Ladle the stew into bowls and serve hot.

Per Serving

calories: 334 | fat: 8g | protein: 34g | carbs: 30g | sugars: 6g | fiber: 7g | sodium:

Buttercup Squash Soup

Prep time: 15 minutes | Cook time: 10 minutes | Serves 6

2 tablespoons extra-virgin olive oil
1 medium onion, chopped
4 to 5 cups Vegetable Broth or Chicken Bone Broth
1½ pounds buttercup squash, peeled, seeded, and cut into 1-inch chunks
½ teaspoon kosher salt
¼ teaspoon ground white pepper
Whole nutmeg, for grating

1. Set the electric pressure cooker to the Sauté setting. When the pot is hot, pour in the olive oil. 2. Add the onion and sauté for 3 to 5 minutes, until it begins to soften. Hit Cancel. 3. Add the broth, squash, salt, and pepper to the pot and stir. (If you want a thicker soup, use 4 cups of broth. If you want a thinner, drinkable soup, use 5 cups.) 4. Close and lock the lid of the pressure cooker. Set the valve to sealing. 5. Cook on high pressure for 10 minutes. 6. When the cooking is complete, hit Cancel and allow the pressure to release naturally. 7. Once the pin drops, unlock and remove the lid. 8. Use an immersion blender to purée the soup right in the pot. If you don't have an immersion blender, transfer the soup to a blender or food processor and purée. (Follow the instructions that came with your machine for blending hot foods.) 9. Pour the soup into serving bowls and grate nutmeg on top.

Turkey Barley Vegetable Soup

Prep time: 5 minutes | Cook time: 20 minutes | Serves 8

2 tablespoons avocado oil
1 pound ground turkey
4 cups Chicken Bone Broth, low-sodium store-bought chicken broth, or water
1 (28-ounce) carton or can diced tomatoes
2 tablespoons tomato paste
1 (15-ounce) package frozen chopped carrots (about 2½ cups)
1 (15-ounce) package frozen peppers and onions (about 2½ cups)
⅓ cup dry barley
1 teaspoon kosher salt
¼ teaspoon freshly ground black pepper
2 bay leaves

1. Set the electric pressure cooker to the Sauté/More setting. When the pot is hot, pour in the avocado oil. 2. Add the turkey to the pot and sauté, stirring frequently to break up the meat, for about 7 minutes or until the turkey is no longer pink. Hit Cancel. 3. Add the broth, tomatoes and their juices, and tomato paste. Stir in the carrots, peppers and onions, barley, salt, pepper, and bay leaves. 4. Close and lock the lid of the pressure cooker. Set the valve to sealing. 5. Cook on high pressure for 20 minutes. 6. When the cooking is complete, hit Cancel and allow the pressure to release naturally for 10 minutes, then quick release any remaining pressure. 7. Once the pin drops, unlock and remove the lid. Discard the bay leaves. 8. Spoon into bowls and serve.

Hot and Sour Soup

Prep time: 10 minutes | Cook time: 30 minutes | Serves 6

4 cups boiling water

1 ounce dried shiitake mushrooms

2 tablespoons cold-pressed avocado oil

3 garlic cloves, chopped

4 ounces cremini or button mushrooms, sliced

1 pound boneless pork loin, sirloin, or tip, thinly sliced against the grain into ¼-inch-thick, ½-inch-wide, 2-inch-long strips

1 teaspoon ground ginger

½ teaspoon ground white pepper

2 cups low-sodium chicken broth or vegetable broth

One 8-ounce can sliced bamboo shoots, drained and rinsed

2 tablespoons low-sodium soy sauce

1 tablespoon chile garlic sauce

1 teaspoon toasted sesame oil

2 teaspoons Lakanto Monkfruit Sweetener Classic

2 large eggs

¼ cup rice vinegar

2 tablespoons cornstarch

4 green onions, white and green parts, thinly sliced

¼ cup chopped fresh cilantro

1. In a large liquid measuring cup or heatproof bowl, pour the boiling water over the shiitake mushrooms. Cover and let soak for 30 minutes. Drain the mushrooms, reserving the soaking liquid. Remove and discard the stems and thinly slice the caps. 2. Select the Sauté setting on the Instant Pot and heat the avocado oil and garlic for 2 minutes, until the garlic is bubbling but not browned. Add the cremini and shiitake mushrooms and sauté for 3 minutes, until the mushrooms are beginning to wilt. Add the pork, ginger, and white pepper and sauté for about 5 minutes, until the pork is opaque and cooked through. 3. Pour

the mushroom soaking liquid into the pot, being careful to leave behind any sediment at the bottom of the measuring cup or bowl. Using a wooden spoon, nudge any browned bits from the bottom of the pot. Stir in the broth, bamboo shoots, soy sauce, chile garlic sauce, sesame oil, and sweetener. 4. Secure the lid and set the Pressure Release to Sealing. Press the Cancel button to reset the cooking program, then select the Pressure Cook or Manual setting and set the cooking time for 5 minutes at high pressure. (The pot will take about 10 minutes to come up to pressure before the cooking program begins.) 5. While the soup is cooking, in a small bowl, beat the eggs until no streaks of yolk remain. 6. When the cooking program ends, let the pressure release naturally for at least 15 minutes, then move the Pressure Release to Venting to release any remaining steam. 7. In a small bowl, stir together the vinegar and cornstarch until the cornstarch dissolves. Open the pot and stir the vinegar mixture into the soup. Press the Cancel button to reset the cooking program, then select the Sauté setting. Bring the soup to a simmer and cook, stirring occasionally, for about 3 minutes, until slightly thickened. While stirring the soup constantly, pour in the beaten eggs in a thin stream. Press the Cancel button to turn off the pot and then stir in the green onions and cilantro. 8. Ladle the soup into bowls and serve hot.

Per Serving

calories: 231 | fat: 13g | protein: 21g | carbs: 14g | sugars: 2g | fiber: 3g | sodium: 250mg

French Market Soup

Prep time: 20 minutes | Cook time: 1 hour | Serves 8

2 cups mixed dry beans, washed with stones removed	16-ounce can low-sodium tomatoes
7 cups water	1 large onion, chopped
1 ham hock, all visible fat removed	1 garlic clove, minced
1 teaspoon salt	1 chile, chopped, or 1 teaspoon chili powder
¼ teaspoon pepper	¼ cup lemon juice

1. Combine all ingredients in the inner pot of the Instant Pot. 2. Secure the lid and make sure vent is set to sealing. Using Manual, set the Instant Pot to cook for 60 minutes. 3. When cooking time is over, let the pressure release naturally. When the Instant Pot is ready, unlock the lid, then remove the bone and any hard or fatty pieces. Pull the meat off the bone and chop into small pieces. Add the

ham back into the Instant Pot.

Per Serving

calories: 191 | fat: 4g | protein: 12g | carbs: 29g | sugars: 5g | fiber: 7g | sodium: 488mg

Ground Turkey Stew

Prep time: 5 minutes | Cook time: 25 minutes | Serves 5

1 tablespoon olive oil	1 green pepper, chopped
1 onion, chopped	1 red pepper, chopped
1 pound ground turkey	1 tomato, chopped
½ teaspoon garlic powder	1½ cups reduced-sodium tomato
1 teaspoon chili powder	sauce
¾ teaspoon cumin	1 tablespoon low-sodium soy sauce
2 teaspoons coriander	1 cup water
1 teaspoon dried oregano	2 handfuls cilantro, chopped
½ teaspoon salt	15-ounce can reduced-salt black beans

1. Press the Sauté function on the control panel of the Instant Pot. 2. Add the olive oil to the inner pot and let it get hot. Add onion and sauté for a few minutes, or until light golden. 3. Add ground turkey. Break the ground meat using a wooden spoon to avoid formation of lumps. Sauté for a few minutes, until the pink color has faded. 4. Add garlic powder, chili powder, cumin, coriander, dried oregano, and salt. Combine well. Add green pepper, red pepper, and chopped tomato. Combine well. 5. Add tomato sauce, soy sauce, and water; combine well. 6. Close and secure the lid. Click on the Cancel key to cancel the Sauté mode. Make sure the pressure release valve on the lid is in the sealing position. 7. Click on Manual function first and then select high pressure. Click the + button and set the time to 15 minutes. 8. You can either have the steam release naturally (it will take around 20 minutes) or, after 10 minutes, turn the pressure release valve on the lid to venting and release steam. Be careful as the steam is very hot. After the pressure has released completely, open the lid. 9. If the stew is watery, turn on the Sauté function and let it cook for a few more minutes with the lid off. 10. Add cilantro and can of black beans, combine well, and let cook for a few minutes.

Per Serving

calories: 209 | fat: 3g | protein: 24g | carbs: 21g | sugars: 8g | fiber: 6g | sodium: 609mg

Chicken Vegetable Soup

Prep time: 12 to 25 minutes | Cook time: 4 minutes | Serves 6

1–2 raw chicken breasts, cubed	1 cup frozen green beans (bite-sized)
½ medium onion, chopped	¼–½ cup chopped savoy cabbage
4 cloves garlic, minced	14½-ounce can low-sodium petite
½ sweet potato, small cubes	diced tomatoes
1 large carrot, peeled and cubed	3 cups low-sodium chicken bone broth
4 stalks celery, chopped, leaves	½ teaspoon black pepper
included	1 teaspoon garlic powder
½ cup frozen corn	¼ cup chopped fresh parsley
¼ cup frozen peas	¼–½ teaspoon red pepper flakes
¼ cup frozen lima beans	

1. Add all of the ingredients, in the order listed, to the inner pot of the Instant Pot. 2. Lock the lid in place, set the vent to sealing, press Manual, and cook at high pressure for 4 minutes. 3. Release the pressure manually as soon as cooking time is finished.

Per Serving

calories: 176 | fat: 3g | protein: 21g | carbs: 18g | sugars: 7g | fiber: 4g | sodium: 169mg

Nancy's Vegetable Beef Soup

Prep time: 25 minutes | Cook time: 8 hours | Serves 8

2-pound roast, cubed, or 2 pounds	tomatoes
stewing meat	5 teaspoons salt-free beef bouillon
15-ounce can corn	powder
15-ounce can green beans	Tabasco, to taste
1-pound bag frozen peas	½ teaspoons salt
40-ounce can no-added-salt stewed	

1. Combine all ingredients in the Instant Pot. Do not drain vegetables. 2. Add water to fill inner pot only to the fill line. 3. Secure the lid, or use the glass lid and set the Instant Pot on Slow Cook mode, Low for 8 hours, or until meat is tender and vegetables are soft.

Per Serving

calories: 229 | fat: 5g | protein: 23g | carbs: 24g | sugars: 10g | fiber: 6g | sodium: 545mg

Ham and Potato Chowder

Prep time: 25 minutes | Cook time: 8 hour s | Serves 5

5-ounce package scalloped potatoes	4 cups water
Sauce mix from potato package	1 cup chopped celery
1 cup extra-lean, reduced-sodium, cooked ham, cut into narrow strips	⅓ cup chopped onions
	Pepper to taste
4 teaspoons sodium-free bouillon powder	2 cups fat-free half-and-half
	⅓ cup flour

1. Combine potatoes, sauce mix, ham, bouillon powder, water, celery, onions, and pepper in the inner pot of the Instant Pot. 2. Secure the lid and cook using the Slow Cook function on low for 7 hours. 3. Combine half-and-half and flour. Remove the lid and gradually add to the inner pot, blending well. 4. Secure the lid once more and cook on the low Slow Cook function for up to 1 hour more, stirring occasionally until thickened.

Per Serving

calories: 241 | fat: 3g | protein: 11g | carbs: 41g | sugars: 8g | fiber: 3g | sodium: 836mg

Savory Beef Stew with Mushrooms and Turnips

Prep time: 0 minutes | Cook time: 55 minutes | Serves 6

1½ pounds beef stew meat	broth
¾ teaspoon fine sea salt	2 tablespoons Worcestershire sauce
¾ teaspoon freshly ground black pepper	1 tablespoon Dijon mustard
	1 teaspoon dried rosemary, crumbled
1 tablespoon cold-pressed avocado oil	1 bay leaf
3 garlic cloves, minced	3 tablespoons tomato paste
1 yellow onion, diced	8 ounces carrots, cut into 1-inch-thick rounds
2 celery stalks, diced	
8 ounces cremini mushrooms, quartered	1 pound turnips, cut into 1-inch pieces
	1 pound parsnips, halved lengthwise,
1 cup low-sodium roasted beef bone	then cut crosswise into 1-inch pieces

1. Sprinkle the beef all over with the salt and pepper. 2. Select the Sauté setting on the Instant Pot and heat the oil and garlic for 2 minutes, until the garlic is bubbling but not browned. Add the onion, celery, and mushrooms and sauté for 5 minutes, until the onion begins to soften and the mushrooms are giving up their liquid. Stir in the broth, Worcestershire sauce, mustard, rosemary, and bay leaf. Stir in the beef. Add the tomato paste in a dollop on top. Do not stir it in. 3. Secure the lid and set the Pressure Release to Sealing. Press the Cancel button to reset the cooking program, then select the Meat/Stew, Pressure Cook, or Manual setting and set the cooking time for 20 minutes at high pressure. (The pot will take about 10 minutes to come up to pressure before the cooking program begins.) 4. When the cooking program ends, perform a quick pressure release by moving the Pressure Release to Venting, or let the pressure release naturally. Open the pot, remove and discard the bay leaf, and stir in the tomato paste. Place the carrots, turnips, and parsnips on top of the meat. 5. Secure the lid and set the Pressure Release to Sealing. Press the Cancel button to reset the cooking program, then select the Pressure Cook or Manual setting and set the cooking time for 3 minutes at low pressure. (The pot will take about 15 minutes to come up to pressure before the cooking program begins.) 6. When the cooking program ends, perform a quick pressure release by moving the Pressure Release to Venting. Open the pot and stir to combine all of the ingredients. 7. Ladle the stew into bowls and serve hot.

Per Serving

calories: 304 | fat: 8g | protein: 29g | carbs: 30g | sugars: 10g | fiber: 8g | sodium: 490mg

Southwestern Bean Soup with Corn Dumplings

Prep time: 50 minutes | Cook time: 4 to 12 hours | Serves 8

15½-ounce can red kidney beans, rinsed and drained

15½-ounce can black beans, pinto beans, or great northern beans, rinsed and drained

3 cups water

14½-ounce can Mexican-style stewed tomatoes

10-ounce package frozen whole-kernel corn, thawed

1 cup sliced carrots

1 cup chopped onions

4-ounce can chopped green chilies

3 teaspoons sodium-free instant bouillon powder (any flavor)

1–2 teaspoons chili powder

2 cloves garlic, minced

Sauce:

⅓ cup flour

¼ cup yellow cornmeal

1 teaspoon baking powder

Dash of pepper

1 egg white, beaten

2 tablespoons milk

1 tablespoon oil

1. Combine the 11 soup ingredients in inner pot of the Instant Pot. 2. Secure the lid and cook on the Low Slow Cook setting for 10–12 hours or high for 4–5 hours. 3. Make dumplings by mixing together flour, cornmeal, baking powder, and pepper. 4. Combine egg white, milk, and oil. Add to flour mixture. Stir with fork until just combined. 5. At the end of the soup's cooking time, turn the Instant Pot to Slow Cook function high if you don't already have it there. Remove the lid and drop dumpling mixture by rounded teaspoonfuls to make 8 mounds atop the soup. 6. Secure the lid once more and cook for an additional 30 minutes.

Per Serving

calories: 197 | fat: 1g | protein: 9g | carbs: 39g | sugars: 6g | fiber: 8g | sodium: 367mg

Pork Chili

Prep time: 15 minutes | Cook time: 4 hour to 8 minutes | Serves 5

1 pound boneless pork ribs	½ cup chopped onion
2 14½-ounce cans fire-roasted diced tomatoes	1 clove garlic, minced
	1 tablespoon chili powder
4¼-ounce cans diced green chiles, drained	

1. Layer the ingredients into the Instant Pot inner pot in the order given. 2. Secure the lid. Cook on the high Slow Cook function for 4 hours or on low 6–8 hours, or until pork is tender but not dry. 3. Cut up or shred meat. Stir into the chili and serve.

Per Serving

calories: 180 | fat: 7g | protein: 18g | carbs: 12g | sugars: 6g | fiber: 3g | sodium: 495mg

Turkey and Pinto Chili

Prep time: 0 minutes | Cook time: 60 minutes | Serves 8

2 tablespoons cold-pressed avocado oil	4 tablespoons chili powder
4 garlic cloves, diced	2 teaspoons ground cumin
1 large yellow onion, diced	2 teaspoons ground coriander
4 jalapeño chiles, seeded and diced	1 teaspoon dried oregano
2 carrots, diced	1 teaspoon dried sage
4 celery stalks, diced	1 cup low-sodium chicken broth
2 teaspoons fine sea salt	3 cups drained cooked pinto beans, or
2 pounds 93 percent lean ground turkey	two 15-ounce cans pinto beans, drained and rinsed
Two 4-ounce cans fire-roasted diced green chiles	Two 14½-ounce cans no-salt petite diced tomatoes and their liquid
	¼ cup tomato paste

1. Select the Sauté setting on the Instant Pot and heat the oil and garlic for 3 minutes, until the garlic is bubbling but not browned. Add the onion, jalapeños, carrots, celery, and salt and sauté for 5 minutes, until the onion begins to soften. Add the turkey and sauté, using a wooden spoon or spatula to break up the meat as it cooks, for 6 minutes, until cooked through and no streaks of pink remain.

Stir in the green chiles, chili powder, cumin, coriander, oregano, sage, and broth, using a wooden spoon or spatula to nudge any browned bits from the bottom of the pot. 2. Pour in the beans in a layer on top of the turkey. Pour in the tomatoes and their liquid and add the tomato paste in a dollop on top. Do not stir in the beans, tomatoes, or tomato paste. 3. Secure the lid and set the Pressure Release to Sealing. Press the Cancel button to reset the cooking program, then select the Pressure Cook or Manual setting and set the cooking time for 15 minutes at high pressure. (The pot will take about 15 minutes to come up to pressure before the cooking program begins.) 4. When the cooking program ends, let the pressure release naturally for at least 20 minutes, then move the Pressure Release to Venting to release any remaining steam. Open the pot and stir the chili to mix all of the ingredients. 5. Press the Cancel button to reset the cooking program, then select the Sauté setting and set the cooking time for 10 minutes. Allow the chili to reduce and thicken. Do not stir the chili while it is cooking, as this will cause it to sputter more. 6. When the cooking program ends, the pot will turn off. Wearing heat-resistant mitts, remove the inner pot from the housing. Wait for about 2 minutes to allow the chili to stop simmering, then give it a final stir. 7. Ladle the chili into bowls and serve hot.

Per Serving

calories: 354 | fat: 14g | protein: 30g | carbs: 28g | sugars: 6g | fiber: 9g | sodium: 819mg

Pasta e Fagioli with Ground Beef

Prep time: 0 minutes | Cook time: 30 minutes | Serves 8

2 tablespoons extra-virgin olive oil	pepper
4 garlic cloves, minced	1¼ cups chickpea-based elbow pasta
1 yellow onion, diced	or whole-wheat elbow pasta
2 large carrots, diced	1½ cups drained cooked kidney beans,
4 celery stalks, diced	or one 15-ounce can kidney beans,
1½ pounds 95 percent extra-lean	rinsed and drained
ground beef	One 28-ounce can whole San Marzano
4 cups low-sodium vegetable broth	tomatoes and their liquid
2 teaspoons Italian seasoning	2 tablespoons chopped fresh flat-leaf
½ teaspoon freshly ground black	parsley

1. Select the Sauté setting on the Instant Pot and heat the oil and garlic for 2

minutes, until the garlic is bubbling but not browned. Add the onion, carrots, and celery and sauté for 5 minutes, until the onion begins to soften. Add the beef and sauté, using a wooden spoon or spatula to break up the meat as it cooks, for 5 minutes; it's fine if some streaks of pink remain, the beef does not need to be cooked through. 2. Stir in the broth, Italian seasoning, pepper, and pasta, making sure all of the pasta is submerged in the liquid. Add the beans and stir to mix. Add the tomatoes and their liquid, crushing the tomatoes with your hands as you add them to the pot. Do not stir them in. 3. Secure the lid and set the Pressure Release to Sealing. Press the Cancel button to reset the cooking program, then select the Pressure Cook or Manual setting and set the cooking time for 2 minutes at low pressure. (The pot will take about 15 minutes to come up to pressure before the cooking program begins.) 4. When the cooking program ends, let the pressure release naturally for 10 minutes, then move the Pressure Release to Venting to release any remaining steam. Open the pot and stir the soup to mix all of the ingredients. 5. Ladle the soup into bowls, sprinkle with the parsley, and serve right away.

Per Serving

calories: 278 | fat: 9g | protein: 26g | carbs: 25g | sugars: 4g | fiber: 6g | sodium: 624mg

Chapter 8 Vegetarian Mains

Instant Pot Hoppin' John with Skillet Cauli "Rice"

Prep time: 0 minutes | Cook time: 30 minutes | Serves 6

Hoppin' John

1 pound dried black-eyed peas (about 2¼ cups)

8⅔ cups water

1½ teaspoons fine sea salt

2 tablespoons extra-virgin olive oil

2 garlic cloves, minced

8 ounces shiitake mushrooms, stemmed and chopped, or cremini mushrooms, chopped

1 small yellow onion, diced

1 green bell pepper, seeded and diced

2 celery stalks, diced

2 jalapeño chiles, seeded and diced

½ teaspoon smoked paprika

½ teaspoon dried thyme

½ teaspoon dried sage

¼ teaspoon cayenne pepper

2 cups low-sodium vegetable broth

Cauli "Rice"

1 tablespoon vegan buttery spread or unsalted butter

1 pound riced cauliflower

½ teaspoon fine sea salt

2 green onions, white and green parts, sliced

Hot sauce (such as Tabasco or Crystal) for serving

1. To make the Hoppin' John: In a large bowl, combine the black-eyed peas, 8 cups of the water, and 1 teaspoon of the salt and stir to dissolve the salt. Let soak for at least 8 hours or up to overnight. 2. Select the Sauté setting on the Instant Pot and heat the oil and garlic for 3 minutes, until the garlic is bubbling but not browned. Add the mushrooms and the remaining ½ teaspoon salt and sauté for 5 minutes, until the mushrooms have wilted and begun to give up their liquid. Add the onion, bell pepper, celery, and jalapeños and sauté for 4 minutes, until the onion is softened. Add the paprika, thyme, sage, and cayenne and sauté for 1 minute. 3. Drain the black-eyed peas and add them to the pot along with the broth and remaining ⅔ cup water. The liquid should just barely cover the beans. (Add an additional splash of water if needed.) 4. Secure the lid and set the Pressure Release to Sealing. Press the Cancel button to reset the cooking program, then select the Bean/Chili, Pressure Cook, or Manual setting and set the cooking time for 5 minutes at high pressure. (The pot will take about 10 minutes to come up to pressure before the cooking program begins.) 5. When the cooking program ends, let the pressure release naturally for 10 minutes, then move the Pressure

Release to Venting to release any remaining steam. 6. To make the cauli "rice": While the pressure is releasing, in a large skillet over medium heat, melt the buttery spread. Add the cauliflower and salt and sauté for 3 to 5 minutes, until cooked through and piping hot. (If using frozen riced cauliflower, this may take another 2 minutes or so.) 7. Spoon the cauli "rice" onto individual plates. Open the pot and spoon the black-eyed peas on top of the cauli "rice". Sprinkle with the green onions and serve right away, with the hot sauce on the side.

Per Serving

calories: 287 | fat: 7g | protein: 23g | carbs: 56g | sugars: 8g | fiber: 24g | sodium: 894mg

Pra Ram Vegetables and Peanut Sauce with Seared Tofu

Prep time: 5 minutes | Cook time: 20 minutes | Serves 4

Peanut Sauce

2 tablespoons cold-pressed avocado oil

2 garlic cloves, minced

½ cup creamy natural peanut butter

½ cup coconut milk

2 tablespoons brown rice syrup

1 tablespoon plus 1 teaspoon soy sauce, tamari, or coconut aminos

¼ cup water

Vegetables

2 carrots, sliced on the diagonal ¼ inch thick

8 ounces zucchini, julienned ¼ inch thick

1 pound broccoli florets

½ small head green cabbage, cut into 1-inch-thick wedges (with core intact so wedges hold together)

Tofu

One 14-ounce package extra-firm tofu, drained

¼ teaspoon fine sea salt

¼ teaspoon freshly ground black pepper

1 tablespoon cornstarch

2 tablespoons coconut oil

1. To make the peanut sauce: In a small saucepan over medium heat, warm the oil and garlic for about 2 minutes, until the garlic is bubbling but not browned. Add the peanut butter, coconut milk, brown rice syrup, soy sauce, and water; stir to combine; and bring to a simmer (this will take about 3 minutes). As soon as the mixture is fully combined and at a simmer, remove from the heat and keep warm. The peanut sauce will keep in an airtight container in the refrigerator for up to 5 days. 2. To make the vegetables: Pour 1 cup water into the Instant Pot and place a steamer basket into the pot. In order, layer the carrots, zucchini, broccoli, and

cabbage in the steamer basket, finishing with the cabbage. 3. Secure the lid and set the Pressure Release to Sealing. Select the Steam setting and set the cooking time for 0 (zero) minutes at low pressure. (The pot will take about 15 minutes to come up to pressure before the cooking program begins.) 4. To prepare the tofu: While the vegetables are steaming, cut the tofu crosswise into eight ½-inch-thick slices. Cut each of the slices in half crosswise, creating squares. Sandwich the squares between double layers of paper towels or a folded kitchen towel and press firmly to wick away as much moisture as possible. Sprinkle the tofu squares on both sides with the salt and pepper, then sprinkle them on both sides with the cornstarch. Using your fingers, spread the cornstarch on the top and bottom of each square to coat evenly. 5. In a large nonstick skillet over medium-high heat, warm the oil for about 3 minutes, until shimmering. Add the tofu and sear, turning once, for about 6 minutes per side, until crispy and golden. Divide the tofu evenly among four plates. 6. When the cooking program ends, perform a quick pressure release by moving the Pressure Release to Venting. Open the pot and, wearing heat-resistant mitts, grasp the handles of the steamer basket and lift it out of the pot. 7. Divide the vegetables among the plates, arranging them around the tofu. Spoon the peanut sauce over the tofu and serve.

Per Serving

calories: 380 | fat: 22g | protein: 18g | carbs: 30g | sugars: 9g | fiber: 10g | sodium: 381mg

Palak Tofu

Prep time: 5 minutes | Cook time: 40 minutes | Serves 4

1 (14-ounce) package extra-firm tofu, drained

5 tablespoons cold-pressed avocado oil

1 yellow onion, diced

1-inch piece fresh ginger, peeled and minced

3 garlic cloves, minced

1 teaspoon fine sea salt

½ teaspoon freshly ground black pepper

¼ teaspoon cayenne pepper

One 16-ounce bag frozen chopped spinach

⅓ cup water

One 14½-ounce can fire-roasted diced tomatoes and their liquid

¼ cup coconut milk

2 teaspoons garam masala

Cooked brown rice or cauliflower "rice" or whole-grain flatbread for serving

1. Cut the tofu crosswise into eight ½-inch-thick slices. Sandwich the slices between double layers of paper towels or a folded kitchen towel and press firmly to wick away as much moisture as possible. Cut the slices into ½-inch cubes. 2. Select the Sauté setting on the Instant Pot and and heat 4 tablespoons of the oil for 2 minutes. Add the onion and sauté for about 10 minutes, until it begins to brown. 3. While the onion is cooking in the Instant Pot, in a large nonstick skillet over medium-high heat, warm the remaining 1 tablespoon oil. Add the tofu in a single layer and cook without stirring for about 3 minutes, until lightly browned. 4. Using a spatula, turn the cubes over and cook for about 3 minutes more, until browned on the other side. Remove from the heat and set aside. 5. Add the ginger and garlic to the onion in the Instant Pot and sauté for about 2 minutes, until the garlic is bubbling but not browned. Add the sautéed tofu, salt, black pepper, and cayenne and stir gently to combine, taking care not to break up the tofu. Add the spinach and stir gently. Pour in the water and then pour the tomatoes and their liquid over the top in an even layer. Do not stir them in. 6. Secure the lid and set the Pressure Release to Sealing. Press the Cancel button to reset the cooking program, then select the Manual or Pressure Cook setting and set the cooking time for 10 minutes at low pressure. (The pot will take about 15 minutes to come up to pressure before the cooking program begins.) 7. When the cooking program ends, let the pressure release naturally for 10 minutes, then move the Pressure Release to Venting to release any remaining steam. Open the pot, add the coconut milk and garam masala, and stir to combine. 8. Ladle the tofu onto plates or into bowls. Serve piping hot, with the "rice" alongside.

Per Serving

calories: 345 | fat: 24g | protein: 14g | carbs: 18g | sugars: 5g | fiber: 6g | sodium: 777 mg

Vegan Dal Makhani

Prep time: 0 minutes | Cook time: 55 minutes | Serves 6

1 cup dried kidney beans
⅓ cup urad dal or beluga or Puy lentils
4 cups water
1 teaspoon fine sea salt
1 tablespoon cold-pressed avocado oil
1 tablespoon cumin seeds
1-inch piece fresh ginger, peeled and minced
4 garlic cloves, minced
1 large yellow onion, diced
2 jalapeño chiles, seeded and diced

1 green bell pepper, seeded and diced
1 tablespoon garam masala
1 teaspoon ground turmeric
¼ teaspoon cayenne pepper (optional)
One 15-ounce can fire-roasted diced tomatoes and liquid
2 tablespoons vegan buttery spread
Cooked cauliflower "rice" for serving
2 tablespoons chopped fresh cilantro
6 tablespoons plain coconut yogurt

1. In a medium bowl, combine the kidney beans, urad dal, water, and salt and stir to dissolve the salt. Let soak for 12 hours. 2. Select the Sauté setting on the Instant Pot and heat the oil and cumin seeds for 3 minutes, until the seeds are bubbling, lightly toasted, and aromatic. Add the ginger and garlic and sauté for 1 minute, until bubbling and fragrant. Add the onion, jalapeños, and bell pepper and sauté for 5 minutes, until the onion begins to soften. 3. Add the garam masala, turmeric, cayenne (if using), and the soaked beans and their liquid and stir to mix. Pour the tomatoes and their liquid on top. Do not stir them in. 4. Secure the lid and set the Pressure Release to Sealing. Press the Cancel button to reset the cooking program, then select the Pressure Cook or Manual setting and set the cooking time for 30 minutes at high pressure. (The pot will take about 15 minutes to come up to pressure before the cooking program begins.) 5. When the cooking program ends, let the pressure release naturally for 30 minutes, then move the Pressure Release to Venting to release any remaining steam. Open the pot and stir to combine, then stir in the buttery spread. If you prefer a smoother texture, ladle 1½ cups of the dal into a blender and blend until smooth, about 30 seconds, then stir the blended mixture into the rest of the dal in the pot. 6. Spoon the cauliflower "rice" into bowls and ladle the dal on top. Sprinkle with the cilantro, top with a dollop of coconut yogurt, and serve.

Per Serving

Calorie: 245 | fat: 7g | protein: 11g | carbs: 37g | sugars: 4g | fiber: 10g | sodium: 518mg

No-Bake Spaghetti Squash Casserole

Prep time: 10 minutes | Cook time: 45 minutes | Serves 6

Marinara

3 tablespoons extra-virgin olive oil

3 garlic cloves, minced

One 28-ounce can whole San Marzano tomatoes and their liquid

2 teaspoons Italian seasoning

1 teaspoon fine sea salt

½ teaspoon red pepper flakes (optional)

Vegan Parmesan

½ cup raw whole cashews

2 tablespoons nutritional yeast

½ teaspoon garlic powder

½ teaspoon fine sea salt

Vegan Ricotta

One 14-ounce package firm tofu, drained

½ cup raw whole cashews, soaked in water to cover for 1 to 2 hours and then drained

3 tablespoons nutritional yeast

2 tablespoons extra-virgin olive oil

1 teaspoon finely grated lemon zest, plus 2 tablespoons fresh lemon juice

½ cup firmly packed fresh flat-leaf parsley leaves

1½ teaspoons Italian seasoning

1 teaspoon garlic powder

1 teaspoon fine sea salt

½ teaspoon freshly ground black pepper

One 3½-pound steamed spaghetti squash

2 tablespoons chopped fresh flat-leaf parsley

1. To make the marinara: Select the Sauté setting on the Instant Pot and heat the oil and garlic for about 2 minutes, until the garlic is bubbling but not browned. Add the tomatoes and their liquid and use a wooden spoon or spatula to crush the tomatoes against the side of the pot. Stir in the Italian seasoning, salt, and pepper flakes (if using) and cook, stirring occasionally, for about 10 minutes, until the sauce has thickened a bit. Press the Cancel button to turn off the pot and let the sauce cook from the residual heat for about 5 minutes more, until it is no longer simmering. Wearing heat-resistant mitts, lift the pot out of the housing, pour the sauce into a medium heatproof bowl, and set aside. (You can make the sauce up to 4 days in advance, then let it cool, transfer it to an airtight container, and refrigerate.) 2. To make the vegan Parmesan: In a food processor, combine the cashews, nutritional yeast, garlic powder, and salt. Using 1-second pulses, pulse

about ten times, until the mixture resembles grated Parmesan cheese. Transfer to a small bowl and set aside. Do not wash the food processor bowl and blade. 3. To make the vegan ricotta: Cut the tofu crosswise into eight ½-inch-thick slices. Sandwich the slices between double layers of paper towels or a folded kitchen towel and press gently to remove excess moisture. Add the tofu to the food processor along with the cashews, nutritional yeast, oil, lemon zest, lemon juice, parsley, Italian seasoning, garlic powder, salt, and pepper. Process for about 1 minute, until the mixture is mostly smooth with flecks of parsley throughout. Set aside. 4. Return the marinara to the pot. Select the Sauté setting and heat the marinara sauce for about 3 minutes, until it starts to simmer. Add the spaghetti squash and vegan ricotta to the pot and stir to combine. Continue to heat, stirring often, for 8 to 10 minutes, until piping hot. Press the Cancel button to turn off the pot. 5. Spoon the spaghetti squash into bowls, top with the vegan Parmesan and parsley, and serve right away.

Per Serving

Calorie: 307 | fat: 17g | protein: 16g | carbs: 25g | sugars: 2g | fiber: 5g | sodium: 985 mg

Spinach Salad with Eggs, Tempeh Bacon, and Strawberries

Prep time: 10 minutes | Cook time: 15 minutes | Serves 4

2 tablespoons soy sauce, tamari, or coconut aminos	1 shallot, minced
	1 tablespoon red wine vinegar
1 tablespoon raw apple cider vinegar	1 tablespoon balsamic vinegar
1 tablespoon pure maple syrup	1 teaspoon Dijon mustard
½ teaspoon smoked paprika	¼ teaspoon fine sea salt
Freshly ground black pepper	One 6-ounce bag baby spinach
One 8-ounce package tempeh, cut crosswise into ⅛-inch-thick slices	2 hearts romaine lettuce, torn into bite-size pieces
8 large eggs	12 fresh strawberries, sliced
3 tablespoons extra-virgin olive oil	

1. In a 1-quart ziplock plastic bag, combine the soy sauce, cider vinegar, maple syrup, paprika, and ½ teaspoon pepper and carefully agitate the bag to mix the ingredients to make a marinade. Add the tempeh, seal the bag, and turn the bag back and forth several times to coat the tempeh evenly with the marinade. Marinate in the refrigerator for at least 2 hours or up to 24 hours. 2. Pour 1 cup

water into the Instant Pot and place the wire metal steam rack, an egg rack, or a steamer basket into the pot. Gently place the eggs on top of the rack or in the basket, taking care not to crack them. 3. Secure the lid and set the Pressure Release to Sealing. Select the Steam setting and set the cooking time for 3 minutes at high pressure. (The pot will take about 5 minutes to come up to pressure before the cooking program begins.) 4. While the eggs are cooking, prepare an ice bath. 5. When the cooking program ends, perform a quick pressure release by moving the Pressure Release to Venting. Open the pot and, using tongs, transfer the eggs to the ice bath to cool. 6. Remove the tempeh from the marinade and blot dry between layers of paper towels. Discard the marinade. In a large nonstick skillet over medium-high heat, warm 1 tablespoon of the oil for 2 minutes. Add the tempeh in a single layer and fry, turning once, for 2 to 3 minutes per side, until well browned. Transfer the tempeh to a plate and set aside. 7. Wipe out the skillet and set it over medium heat. Add the remaining 2 tablespoons oil and the shallot and sauté for about 2 minutes, until the shallot is golden brown. Turn off the heat and stir in the red wine vinegar, balsamic vinegar, mustard, salt, and ¼ teaspoon pepper to make a vinaigrette. 8. In a large bowl, combine the spinach and romaine. Pour in the vinaigrette and toss until all of the leaves are lightly coated. Divide the dressed greens evenly among four large serving plates or shallow bowls and arrange the strawberries and fried tempeh on top. Peel the eggs, cut them in half lengthwise, and place them on top of the salads. Top with a couple grinds of pepper and serve right away.

Per Serving

Calorie: 435 | fat: 25g | protein: 29g | carbs: 25g | sugars: 10g | fiber: 5g | sodium: 332mg

86. Chile Relleno Casserole with Salsa Salad

Prep time: 10 minutes | Cook time: 55 minutes | Serves 4

Casserole

½ cup gluten-free flour (such as King Arthur or Cup4Cup brand)

1 teaspoon baking powder

6 large eggs

½ cup nondairy milk or whole milk

Three 4-ounce cans fire-roasted diced green chiles, drained

1 cup nondairy cheese shreds or shredded mozzarella cheese

Salad

1 head green leaf lettuce, shredded

2 Roma tomatoes, seeded and diced

1 green bell pepper, seeded and diced

½ small yellow onion, diced

1 jalapeño chile, seeded and diced (optional)

2 tablespoons chopped fresh cilantro

4 teaspoons extra-virgin olive oil

4 teaspoons fresh lime juice

⅛ teaspoon fine sea salt

1. To make the casserole: Pour 1 cup water into the Instant Pot. Butter a 7-cup round heatproof glass dish or coat with nonstick cooking spray and place the dish on a long-handled silicone steam rack. (If you don't have the long-handled rack, use the wire metal steam rack and a homemade sling) 2. In a medium bowl, whisk together the flour and baking powder. Add the eggs and milk and whisk until well blended, forming a batter. Stir in the chiles and ¾ cup of the cheese. 3. Pour the batter into the prepared dish and cover tightly with aluminum foil. Holding the handles of the steam rack, lower the dish into the Instant Pot. 4. Secure the lid and set the Pressure Release to Sealing. Select the Pressure Cook or Manual setting and set the cooking time for 40 minutes at high pressure. (The pot will take about 10 minutes to come up to pressure before the cooking program begins.) 5. When the cooking program ends, let the pressure release naturally for at least 10 minutes, then move the Pressure Release to Venting to release any remaining steam. Open the pot and, wearing heat-resistant mitts, grasp the handles of the steam rack and lift it out of the pot. Uncover the dish, taking care not to get burned by the steam or to drip condensation onto the casserole. While the casserole is still piping hot, sprinkle the remaining ¼ cup cheese evenly on top. Let the cheese melt for 5 minutes. 6. To make the salad: While the cheese is melting, in a large bowl, combine the lettuce, tomatoes, bell pepper, onion, jalapeño (if using), cilantro, oil, lime juice, and salt. Toss until evenly combined. 7. Cut the casserole into wedges. Serve warm, with the salad on

the side.
Per Serving
Calorie: 361 | fat: 22g | protein: 21g | carbs: 23g | sugars: 8g | fiber: 3g | sodium: 421 mg

Chapter 9 Desserts

Crustless Key Lime Cheesecake

Prep time: 15 minutes | Cook time: 35 minutes | Serves 8

Nonstick cooking spray	Lime Juice)
16 ounces light cream cheese (Neufchâtel), softened	½ teaspoon vanilla extract
	¼ cup plain Greek yogurt
⅔ cup granulated erythritol sweetener	1 teaspoon grated lime zest
¼ cup unsweetened Key lime juice (I like Nellie & Joe's Famous Key West	2 large eggs
	Whipped cream, for garnish (optional)

1. Spray a 7-inch springform pan with nonstick cooking spray. Line the bottom and partway up the sides of the pan with foil. 2. Put the cream cheese in a large bowl. Use an electric mixer to whip the cream cheese until smooth, about 2 minutes. Add the erythritol, lime juice, vanilla, yogurt, and zest, and blend until smooth. Stop the mixer and scrape down the sides of the bowl with a rubber spatula. With the mixer on low speed, add the eggs, one at a time, blending until just mixed. (Don't overbeat the eggs.) 3. Pour the mixture into the prepared pan. Drape a paper towel over the top of the pan, not touching the cream cheese mixture, and tightly wrap the top of the pan in foil. (Your goal here is to keep out as much moisture as possible.) 4. Pour 1 cup of water into the electric pressure cooker. 5. Place the foil-covered pan onto the wire rack and carefully lower it into the pot. 6. Close and lock the lid of the pressure cooker. Set the valve to sealing. 7. Cook on high pressure for 35 minutes. 8. When the cooking is complete, hit Cancel. Allow the pressure to release naturally for 20 minutes, then quick release any remaining pressure. 9. Once the pin drops, unlock and remove the lid. 10. Using the handles of the wire rack, carefully transfer the pan to a cooling rack. Cool to room temperature, then refrigerate for at least 3 hours. 11. When ready to serve, run a thin rubber spatula around the rim of the cheesecake to loosen it, then remove the ring. 12. Slice into wedges and serve with whipped cream (if

using).

Fudgy Walnut Brownies

Prep time: 10 minutes | Cook time: 1 hour | Serves 12

¾ cup walnut halves and pieces	Golden
½ cup unsalted butter, melted and cooled	¼ teaspoon fine sea salt
	¾ cup almond flour
4 large eggs	¾ cup natural cocoa powder
1½ teaspoons instant coffee crystals	¾ cup stevia-sweetened chocolate chips
1½ teaspoons vanilla extract	
1 cup Lakanto Monkfruit Sweetener	

1. In a dry small skillet over medium heat, toast the walnuts, stirring often, for about 5 minutes, until golden. Transfer the walnuts to a bowl to cool. 2. Pour 1 cup water into the Instant Pot. Line the base of a 7 by 3-inch round cake pan with a circle of parchment paper. Butter the sides of the pan and the parchment or coat with nonstick cooking spray. 3. Pour the butter into a medium bowl. One at a time, whisk in the eggs, then whisk in the coffee crystals, vanilla, sweetener, and salt. Finally, whisk in the flour and cocoa powder just until combined. Using a rubber spatula, fold in the chocolate chips and walnuts. 4. Transfer the batter to the prepared pan and, using the spatula, spread it in an even layer. Cover the pan tightly with aluminum foil. Place the pan on a long-handled silicone steam rack, then, holding the handles of the steam rack, lower it into the Instant Pot. 5. Secure the lid and set the Pressure Release to Sealing. Select the Cake, Pressure Cook, or Manual setting and set the cooking time for 45 minutes at high pressure. (The pot will take about 10 minutes to come up to pressure before the cooking program begins.) 6. When the cooking program ends, let the pressure release naturally for 10 minutes, then move the Pressure Release to Venting to release any remaining steam. Open the pot and, wearing heat-resistant mitts, grasp the handles of the steam rack and lift it out of the pot. Uncover the pan, taking care not to get burned by the steam or to drip condensation onto the brownies. Let the brownies cool in the pan on a cooling rack for about 2 hours, to room temperature. 7. Run a butter knife around the edge of the pan to make sure the brownies are not sticking to the pan sides. Invert the brownies onto the rack, lift off the pan, and peel off the parchment paper. Invert the brownies onto a serving plate and cut into twelve wedges. The brownies will keep, stored in an airtight

container in the refrigerator for up to 5 days, or in the freezer for up to 4 months.

Per Serving

calories: 199 | fat: 19g | protein: 5g | carbs: 26g | sugars: 10g | fiber: 20g | sodium: 56mg

Almond Butter Blondies

Prep time: 10 minutes | Cook time: 20 minutes | Serves 8

½ cup creamy natural almond butter, at room temperature

4 large eggs

¾ cup Lakanto Monkfruit Sweetener Golden

1 teaspoon pure vanilla extract

½ teaspoon fine sea salt

1¼ cups almond flour

¾ cup stevia-sweetened chocolate chips

1. Pour 1 cup water into the Instant Pot. Line the base of a 7 by 3-inch round cake pan with a circle of parchment paper. Butter the sides of the pan and the parchment or coat with nonstick cooking spray. 2. Put the almond butter into a medium bowl. One at a time, whisk the eggs into the almond butter, then whisk in the sweetener, vanilla, and salt. Stir in the flour just until it is fully incorporated, followed by the chocolate chips. 3. Transfer the batter to the prepared pan and, using a rubber spatula, spread it in an even layer. Cover the pan tightly with aluminum foil. Place the pan on a long-handled silicone steam rack, then, holding the handles of the steam rack, lower it into the Instant Pot. 4. Secure the lid and set the Pressure Release to Sealing. Select the Cake, Pressure Cook, or Manual setting and set the cooking time for 40 minutes at high pressure. (The pot will take about 10 minutes to come up to pressure before the cooking program begins.) 5. When the cooking program ends, let the pressure release naturally for 10 minutes, then move the Pressure Release to Venting to release any remaining steam. Open the pot and, wearing heat-resistant mitts, grasp the handles of the steam rack and lift it out of the pot. Uncover the pan, taking care not to get burned by the steam or to drip condensation onto the blondies. Let the blondies cool in the pan on a cooling rack for about 5 minutes. 6. Run a butter knife around the edge of pan to make sure the blondies are not sticking to the pan sides. Invert the blondies onto the rack, lift off the pan, and peel off the parchment paper. Let cool for 15 minutes, then invert the blondies onto a serving

plate and cut into eight wedges. The blondies will keep, stored in an airtight container in the refrigerator for up to 5 days, or in the freezer for up to 4 months.

Per Serving

calories: 211 | fat: 17g | protein: 8g | carbs: 20g | sugars: 10g | fiber: 17g | sodium: 186mg

Greek Yogurt Strawberry Pops

Prep time: 5 minutes | Cook time: 0 minutes | Serves 6

2 ripe bananas, peeled, cut into ½-inch pieces, and frozen
½ cup plain 2 percent Greek yogurt
1 cup chopped fresh strawberries

1. In a food processor, combine the bananas and yogurt and process at high speed for 2 minutes, until mostly smooth (it's okay if a few small chunks remain). Scrape down the sides of the bowl, add the strawberries, and process for 1 minute, until smooth. 2. Divide the mixture evenly among six ice-pop molds. Tap each mold on a countertop a few times to get rid of any air pockets, then place an ice-pop stick into each mold and transfer the molds to the freezer. Freeze for at least 4 hours, or until frozen solid. 3. To unmold each ice pop, run it under cold running water for 5 seconds, taking care not to get water inside the mold, then remove the ice pop from the mold. Eat the ice pops right away or store in a ziplock plastic freezer bag in the freezer for up to 2 months.

Per Serving

calories: 57 | fat: 1g | protein: 3g | carbs: 12g | sugars: 6g | fiber: 2g | sodium: 8mg

Low-Sodium Chicken Broth

Prep time: 5 minutes | Cook time: 1 hour 5 minutes | Makes 8 cups

2½ pounds bony chicken parts (such as drumsticks, wings, necks, and backs)	1 yellow onion, cut into wedges
	6 flat-leaf parsley sprigs
	1¼ teaspoons fine sea salt
2 celery stalks, cut into 3-inch lengths	½ teaspoon poultry seasoning
2 carrots, halved lengthwise, then cut crosswise into 3-inch lengths	2 teaspoons raw apple cider vinegar
	8 cups water

1. Combine the chicken parts, celery, carrots, onion, parsley, salt, and poultry seasoning in the Instant Pot. Add the vinegar and water, pouring slowly to prevent splashing. Make sure the pot is no more than two-thirds full. 2. Secure the lid and set the Pressure Release to Sealing. Select the Soup/Broth, Pressure Cook, or Manual setting and set the cooking time for 40 minutes at high pressure. (The pot will take about 25 minutes to come up to pressure before the cooking program begins.) 3. When the cooking program ends, let the pressure release naturally for at least 40 minutes, then move the Pressure Release to Venting to release any remaining steam. 4. Place a fine-mesh strainer over a large heatproof bowl or pitcher. For a clearer broth, line the strainer with a double layer of cheesecloth. 5. Open the pot and, using tongs, remove and discard the chicken pieces. Wearing heat-resistant mitts, lift out the inner pot and pour the broth through the strainer. Discard the contents of the strainer. Pour the broth into a fat separator to remove the fat, then let the broth cool to room temperature. Alternatively, let the broth cool to room temperature, then chill in the refrigerator until the fat solidifies on top and scoop off the fat from the surface with a large spoon. (To speed up the cooling process, prepare an ice bath and set the bowl in the ice bath for about 15 minutes.) 6. The broth can be used right away, or stored in an airtight container in the refrigerator for up to 5 days or in the freezer for up to 6 months.

Per Serving

calories: 35 | fat: 0g | protein: 8g | carbs: 0g | sugars: 1g | fiber: 0g | sodium: 533mg

Low-Sodium Roasted Beef Bone Broth

Prep time: 15 minutes | Cook time: 3hours 15 minutes | Makes 8 cups

2 pounds beef soup bones (such as knucklebones, shanks, or oxtails)
2 celery stalks, cut into 3-inch lengths
1 parsnip or 2 large carrots, halved lengthwise, then cut crosswise into 3-inch lengths
1 yellow onion, cut into wedges

1 teaspoon fine sea salt
½ teaspoon black peppercorns
2 bay leaves
1 tablespoon tomato paste
1 tablespoon raw apple cider vinegar
8 cups water

1. Preheat the oven to 400°F. Line a large sheet pan with aluminum foil. 2. Arrange the beef bones in a single layer on the prepared pan. Roast for about 45 minutes, until browned. 3. Using tongs, transfer the roasted bones to the Instant Pot. Add the celery, parsnip, onion, salt, peppercorns, bay leaves, tomato paste, and vinegar. Slowly pour in the water to prevent splashing. Make sure the pot is no more than two-thirds full. 4. Secure the lid and set the Pressure Release to Sealing. Select the Soup/Broth, Pressure Cook, or Manual setting and set the cooking time for 120 minutes at high pressure. (The pot will take about 30 minutes to come up to pressure before the cooking program begins.) 5. When the cooking program ends, let the pressure release naturally; this will take about 45 minutes. 6. Place a fine-mesh strainer over a large heatproof bowl or pitcher. For a clearer broth, line the strainer with a double layer of cheesecloth. 7. Open the pot and, using tongs, remove the bones. Wearing heat-resistant mitts, lift out the inner pot and pour the broth through the strainer. Discard the contents of the strainer. You can pick the meat off the bones if you like, but it will have given up most of its flavor to the broth. Pour the broth into a fat separator to remove the fat, then let the broth cool to room temperature. Alternatively, let the broth cool to room temperature, then chill in the refrigerator until the fat solidifies on top and scoop off the fat from the surface with a large spoon. (To speed up the cooling process, prepare an ice bath and set the bowl in the ice bath for about 15 minutes.) 8. The broth can be used right away, or stored in an airtight container in the refrigerator for up to 5 days or in the freezer for up to 6 months.

Per Serving

calories: 30 | fat: 0g | protein: 6g | carbs: 1g | sugars: 1g | fiber: 0g | sodium: 313mg

Cashew Ranch Dip

Prep time: 1 minutes | Cook time: 1 hour | Makes 2 cups

1 cup raw whole cashews, soaked in water to cover for 1 to 2 hours and then drained
½ cup water
2 tablespoons fresh lemon juice
1 teaspoon nutritional yeast
1 teaspoon garlic powder
½ teaspoon fine sea salt
½ teaspoon freshly ground black pepper
1 tablespoon chopped fresh chives
1 tablespoon chopped fresh dill
1 tablespoon chopped fresh flat-leaf parsley

1. In a blender, combine the cashews, water, lemon juice, nutritional yeast, garlic powder, salt, and pepper. Blend on high speed for about 1 minute, until very smooth, stopping to scrape down the sides if needed. 2. Transfer the dip to a bowl and stir in the chives, dill, and parsley. Cover and refrigerate for at least 1 hour before serving. The dip will keep in the refrigerator for up to 5 days. If it becomes too thick, stir in a splash of water.

Per Serving

calories: 44 | fat: 3g | protein: 1g | carbs: 3g | sugars: 0g | fiber: 0g | sodium: 171mg

Cornbread

Prep time: 10 minutes | Cook time: 45 minutes | Serves 8

1 cup almond flour
½ cup cornmeal
¼ cup coconut flour
2 teaspoons baking powder
1 teaspoon fine sea salt
2 large eggs
1 cup unsweetened almond milk
4 tablespoons vegan shortening or unsalted butter, melted and cooled

1. Pour 1 cup water into the Instant Pot. Grease the bottom and sides of a 7-inch round cake pan with shortening or butter. 2. In a medium bowl, whisk together the almond flour, cornmeal, coconut flour, baking powder, and salt. In another

medium bowl, whisk together the eggs and almond milk until no streaks of yolk remain. 3. Add the egg mixture and shortening to the almond flour mixture and whisk just until the dry ingredients are evenly and fully moistened. The coconut flour absorbs moisture quickly, so the batter will thicken as it sits. 4. Transfer the batter to the prepared pan and, using a rubber spatula, spread it in an even layer. Cover the pan tightly with aluminum foil. Place the pan on a long-handled silicone steam rack, then, holding the handles of the steam rack, lower it into the Instant Pot. (If you don't have the long-handled rack, use the wire metal steam rack and a homemade sling) 5. Secure the lid and set the Pressure Release to Sealing. Select the Cake, Pressure Cook, or Manual setting and set the cooking time for 35 minutes at high pressure. (The pot will take about 10 minutes to come up to pressure before the cooking program begins.) 6. When the cooking program ends, let the pressure release naturally for 10 minutes, then move the Pressure Release to Venting to release any remaining steam. Open the pot and, wearing heat-resistant mitts, grasp the handles of the steam rack, lift it out of the pot, and set it on a cooling rack. Uncover the pan, taking care not to get burned by the steam or to drip condensation onto the bread. Let the bread cool for 5 minutes, then run a butter knife around the edge of the pan to loosen the bread from the pan sides. Invert the bread onto the cooling rack, lift off the pan, and invert the bread onto a serving plate. 7. Cut the bread into eight wedges and serve warm.

Per Serving

calories: 230 | fat: 17g | protein: 6g | carbs: 14g | sugars: 1g | fiber: 3g | sodium: 309mg

Chapter 11 Vegetables and Sides

Parmesan-Topped Acorn Squash

Prep time: 10 minutes | Cook time: 20 minutes | Serves 4

1 acorn squash (about 1 pound)	⅛ teaspoon freshly ground black pepper
1 tablespoon extra-virgin olive oil	2 tablespoons freshly grated Parmesan cheese
1 teaspoon dried sage leaves, crumbled	
¼ teaspoon freshly grated nutmeg	
⅛ teaspoon kosher salt	

1. Cut the acorn squash in half lengthwise and remove the seeds. Cut each half in

half for a total of 4 wedges. Snap off the stem if it's easy to do. 2. In a small bowl, combine the olive oil, sage, nutmeg, salt, and pepper. Brush the cut sides of the squash with the olive oil mixture. 3. Pour 1 cup of water into the electric pressure cooker and insert a wire rack or trivet. 4. Place the squash on the trivet in a single layer, skin-side down. 5. Close and lock the lid of the pressure cooker. Set the valve to sealing. 6. Cook on high pressure for 20 minutes. 7. When the cooking is complete, hit Cancel and quick release the pressure. 8. Once the pin drops, unlock and remove the lid. 9. Carefully remove the squash from the pot, sprinkle with the Parmesan, and serve.

Spaghetti Squash

Prep time: 5 minutes | Cook time: 7 minutes | Serves 4
1 spaghetti squash (about 2 pounds)

1. Cut the spaghetti squash in half crosswise and use a large spoon to remove the seeds. 2. Pour 1 cup of water into the electric pressure cooker and insert a wire rack or trivet. 3. Place the squash halves on the rack, cut-side up. 4. Close and lock the lid of the pressure cooker. Set the valve to sealing. 5. Cook on high pressure for 7 minutes. 6. When the cooking is complete, hit Cancel and quick release the pressure. 7. Once the pin drops, unlock and remove the lid. 8. With tongs, remove the squash from the pot and transfer it to a plate. When it is cool enough to handle, scrape the squash with the tines of a fork to remove the strands. Discard the skin.

Parmesan Cauliflower Mash

Prep time: 7 minutes | Cook time: 5 minutes | Serves 4

1 head cauliflower, cored and cut into large florets	¾ cup freshly grated Parmesan cheese
½ teaspoon kosher salt	1 tablespoon unsalted butter or ghee (optional)
½ teaspoon garlic pepper	Chopped fresh chives
2 tablespoons plain Greek yogurt	

1. Pour 1 cup of water into the electric pressure cooker and insert a steamer basket or wire rack. 2. Place the cauliflower in the basket. 3. Close and lock the lid of the pressure cooker. Set the valve to sealing. 4. Cook on high pressure for 5

minutes. 5. When the cooking is complete, hit Cancel and quick release the pressure. 6. Once the pin drops, unlock and remove the lid. 7. Remove the cauliflower from the pot and pour out the water. Return the cauliflower to the pot and add the salt, garlic pepper, yogurt, and cheese. Use an immersion blender or potato masher to purée or mash the cauliflower in the pot. 8. Spoon into a serving bowl, and garnish with butter (if using) and chives.

Per Serving

calories: 141 | fat: 6g | protein: 12g | carbs: 12g | sugars: 9g | fiber: 4g | sodium: 592mg

98.Vegetable Medley

Prep time: 20 minutes | Cook time: 2 minutes | Serves 8

2 medium parsnips	1 teaspoon salt
4 medium carrots	3 tablespoons sugar
1 turnip, about 4½ inches diameter	2 tablespoons canola or olive oil
1 cup water	½ teaspoon salt

1. Clean and peel vegetables. Cut in 1-inch pieces. 2. Place the cup of water and 1 teaspoon salt into the Instant Pot's inner pot with the vegetables. 3. Secure the lid and make sure vent is set to sealing. Press Manual and set for 2 minutes. 4. When cook time is up, release the pressure manually and press Cancel. Drain the water from the inner pot. 5. Press Sauté and stir in sugar, oil, and salt. Cook until sugar is dissolved. Serve.

Per Serving

calories: 63 | fat: 2g | protein: 1g | carbs: 12g | sugars: 6g | fiber: 2g | sodium: 327mg

Caramelized Onions

Prep time: 10 minutes | Cook time: 35 minutes | Serves 8

4 tablespoons margarine
6 large Vidalia or other sweet onions, sliced into thin half rings
10-ounce can chicken, or vegetable, broth

1. Press Sauté on the Instant Pot. Add in the margarine and let melt. 2. Once the margarine is melted, stir in the onions and sauté for about 5 minutes. Pour in the

broth and then press Cancel. 3. Secure the lid and make sure vent is set to sealing. Press Manual and set time for 20 minutes. 4. When cook time is up, release the pressure manually. Remove the lid and press Sauté. Stir the onion mixture for about 10 more minutes, allowing extra liquid to cook off.

Per Serving

Calorie: 123 | fat: 6g | protein: 2g | carbs: 15g | sugars: 10g | fiber: 3g | sodium: 325mg

Perfect Sweet Potatoes

Prep time: 5 minutes | Cook time: 15 minutes | Serves 4 to 6

4–6 medium sweet potatoes
1 cup of water

1. Scrub skin of sweet potatoes with a brush until clean. Pour water into inner pot of the Instant Pot. Place steamer basket in the bottom of the inner pot. Place sweet potatoes on top of steamer basket. 2. Secure the lid and turn valve to seal. 3. Select the Manual mode and set to pressure cook on high for 15 minutes. 4. Allow pressure to release naturally (about 10 minutes). 5. Once the pressure valve lowers, remove lid and serve immediately.

Per Serving

calories: 112 | fat: 0g | protein: 2g | carbs: 26g | sugars: 5g | fiber: 4g | sodium: 72mg

Wild Rice Salad with Cranberries and Almonds

Prep time: 10 minutes | Cook time: 25 minutes | Serves 18

For the rice
2 cups wild rice blend, rinsed
1 teaspoon kosher salt
2½ cups Vegetable Broth or Chicken Bone Broth
For the dressing
¼ cup extra-virgin olive oil
¼ cup white wine vinegar
1½ teaspoons grated orange zest
Juice of 1 medium orange (about ¼ cup)
1 teaspoon honey or pure maple syrup
For the salad
¾ cup unsweetened dried cranberries
½ cup sliced almonds, toasted
Freshly ground black pepper

Make the Rice 1. In the electric pressure cooker, combine the rice, salt, and broth.

2. Close and lock the lid. Set the valve to sealing. 3. Cook on high pressure for 25 minutes. 4. When the cooking is complete, hit Cancel and allow the pressure to release naturally for 15 minutes, then quick release any remaining pressure. 5. Once the pin drops, unlock and remove the lid. 6. Let the rice cool briefly, then fluff it with a fork. Make the Dressing 7. While the rice cooks, make the dressing: In a small jar with a screw-top lid, combine the olive oil, vinegar, zest, juice, and honey. (If you don't have a jar, whisk the ingredients together in a small bowl.) Shake to combine. Make the Salad 8. In a large bowl, combine the rice, cranberries, and almonds. 9. Add the dressing and season with pepper. 10. Serve warm or refrigerate.

Italian Wild Mushrooms

Prep time: 30 minutes | Cook time: 3 minutes | Serves 10

2 tablespoons canola oil	3 fresh bay leaves
2 large onions, chopped	10 fresh basil leaves, chopped
4 garlic cloves, minced	1 teaspoon salt
3 large red bell peppers, chopped	1½ teaspoons pepper
3 large green bell peppers, chopped	28-ounce can Italian plum tomatoes,
12-ounce package oyster mushrooms,	crushed or chopped
cleaned and chopped	

1. Press Sauté on the Instant Pot and add in the oil. Once the oil is heated, add the onions, garlic, peppers, and mushroom to the oil. Sauté just until mushrooms begin to turn brown. 2. Add remaining ingredients. Stir well. 3. Secure the lid and make sure vent is set to sealing. Press Manual and set time for 3 minutes. 4. When cook time is up, release the pressure manually. Discard bay leaves.

Per Serving
calories: 82 | fat: 3g | protein: 3g | carbs: 13g | sugars: 8g | fiber: 4g | sodium: 356 mg

Potatoes with Parsley

Prep time: 10 minutes | Cook time: 5 minutes | Serves 4

3 tablespoons margarine, divided
2 pounds medium red potatoes (about 2 ounces each), halved lengthwise
1 clove garlic, minced

½ teaspoon salt
½ cup low-sodium chicken broth
2 tablespoons chopped fresh parsley

1. Place 1 tablespoon margarine in the inner pot of the Instant Pot and select Sauté. 2. After margarine is melted, add potatoes, garlic, and salt, stirring well. 3. Sauté 4 minutes, stirring frequently. 4. Add chicken broth and stir well. 5. Seal lid, make sure vent is on sealing, then select Manual for 5 minutes on high pressure. 6. When cooking time is up, manually release the pressure. 7. Strain potatoes, toss with remaining 2 tablespoons margarine and chopped parsley, and serve immediately.

Per Serving

calories: 237 | fat: 9g | protein: 5g | carbs: 37g | sugars: 3g | fiber: 4g | sodium: 389mg

Best Brown Rice

Prep time: 5 minutes | Cook time: 22 minutes | Serves 6 to 12

2 cups brown rice

2½ cups water

1. Rinse brown rice in a fine-mesh strainer. 2. Add rice and water to the inner pot of the Instant Pot. 3. Secure the lid and make sure vent is on sealing. 4. Use Manual setting and select 22 minutes cooking time on high pressure. 5. When cooking time is done, let the pressure release naturally for 10 minutes, then press Cancel and manually release any remaining pressure.

Per Serving

Calorie: 114 | fat: 1g | protein: 2g | carbs: 23g | sugars: 0g | fiber: 1g | sodium: 3mg

Appendix 1: Measurement Conversion Chart

VOLUME EQUIVALENTS(DRY)

US STANDARD	METRIC (APPROXIMATE)
1/8 teaspoon	0.5 mL
1/4 teaspoon	1 mL
1/2 teaspoon	2 mL
3/4 teaspoon	4 mL
1 teaspoon	5 mL
1 tablespoon	15 mL
1/4 cup	59 mL
1/2 cup	118 mL
3/4 cup	177 mL
1 cup	235 mL
2 cups	475 mL
3 cups	700 mL
4 cups	1 L

VOLUME EQUIVALENTS(LIQUID)

US STANDARD	US STANDARD (OUNCES)	METRIC (APPROXIMATE)
2 tablespoons	1 fl.oz.	30 mL
1/4 cup	2 fl.oz.	60 mL
1/2 cup	4 fl.oz.	120 mL
1 cup	8 fl.oz.	240 mL
1 1/2 cup	12 fl.oz.	355 mL
2 cups or 1 pint	16 fl.oz.	475 mL
4 cups or 1 quart	32 fl.oz.	1 L
1 gallon	128 fl.oz.	4 L

TEMPERATURES EQUIVALENTS

FAHRENHEIT(F)	CELSIUS(C) (APPROXIMATE)
225 °F	107 °C
250 °F	120 °C
275 °F	135 °C
300 °F	150 °C
325 °F	160 °C
350 °F	180 °C
375 °F	190 °C
400 °F	205 °C
425 °F	220 °C
450 °F	235 °C
475 °F	245 °C
500 °F	260 °C

WEIGHT EQUIVALENTS

US STANDARD	METRIC (APPROXIMATE)
1 ounce	28 g
2 ounces	57 g
5 ounces	142 g
10 ounces	284 g
15 ounces	425 g
16 ounces (1 pound)	455 g
1.5 pounds	680 g
2 pounds	907 g

Appendix 2: Instant Pot Cooking Timetable

Dried Beans, Legumes and Lentils

Dried Beans and Legume	Dry (Minutes)	Soaked (Minutes)
Soy beans	25 – 30	20 – 25
Scarlet runner	20 – 25	10 – 15
Pinto beans	25 – 30	20 – 25
Peas	15 – 20	10 – 15
Navy beans	25 – 30	20 – 25
Lima beans	20 – 25	10 – 15
Lentils, split, yellow (moong dal)	15 – 18	N/A
Lentils, split, red	15 – 18	N/A
Lentils, mini, green (brown)	15 – 20	N/A
Lentils, French green	15 – 20	N/A
Kidney white beans	35 – 40	20 – 25
Kidney red beans	25 – 30	20 – 25
Great Northern beans	25 – 30	20 – 25
Pigeon peas	20 – 25	15 – 20
Chickpeas (garbanzo bean chickpeas)	35 – 40	20 – 25
Cannellini beans	35 – 40	20 – 25
Black-eyed peas	20 – 25	10 – 15
Black beans	20 – 25	10 – 15

Fish and Seafood

Fish and Seafood	Fresh (minutes)	Frozen (minutes)
Shrimp or Prawn	1 to 2	2 to 3
Seafood soup or stock	6 to 7	7 to 9
Mussels	2 to 3	4 to 6
Lobster	3 to 4	4 to 6
Fish, whole (snapper, trout, etc.)	5 to 6	7 to 10
Fish steak	3 to 4	4 to 6
Fish fillet,	2 to 3	3 to 4
Crab	3 to 4	5 to 6

Fruits

Fruits	Fresh (in Minutes)	Dried (in Minutes)
Raisins	N/A	4 to 5
Prunes	2 to 3	4 to 5
Pears, whole	3 to 4	4 to 6
Pears, slices or halves	2 to 3	4 to 5
Peaches	2 to 3	4 to 5
Apricots, whole or halves	2 to 3	3 to 4
Apples, whole	3 to 4	4 to 6
Apples, in slices or pieces	2 to 3	3 to 4

Meat

Meat and Cuts	Cooking Time (minutes)	Meat and Cuts	Cooking Time (minutes)
Veal, roast	35 to 45	Duck, with bones, cut up	10 to 12
Veal, chops	5 to 8	Cornish Hen, whole	10 to 15
Turkey, drumsticks (leg)	15 to 20	Chicken, whole	20 to 25
Turkey, breast, whole, with bones	25 to 30	Chicken, legs, drumsticks, or thighs	10 to 15
Turkey, breast, boneless	15 to 20	Chicken, with bones, cut up	10 to 15
Quail, whole	8 to 10	Chicken, breasts	8 to 10
Pork, ribs	20 to 25	Beef, stew	15 to 20
Pork, loin roast	55 to 60	Beef, shanks	25 to 30
Pork, butt roast	45 to 50	Beef, ribs	25 to 30
Pheasant	20 to 25	Beef, steak, pot roast, round, rump, brisket or blade, small chunks, chuck,	25 to 30
Lamb, stew meat	10 to 15		
Lamb, leg	35 to 45	Beef, pot roast, steak, rump, round, chuck, blade or brisket, large	35 to 40
Lamb, cubes,	10 t0 15		
Ham slice	9 to 12	Beef, ox-tail	40 to 50
Ham picnic shoulder	25 to 30	Beef, meatball	10 to 15
Duck, whole	25 to 30	Beef, dressed	20 to 25

Vegetables (fresh/frozen)

Vegetable	Fresh (minutes)	Frozen (minutes)	Vegetable	Fresh (minutes)	Frozen (minutes)
Zucchini, slices or chunks	2 to 3	3 to 4	Mixed vegetables	2 to 3	3 to 4
Yam, whole, small	10 to 12	12 to 14	Leeks	2 to 4	3 to 5
Yam, whole, large	12 to 15	15 to 19	Greens (collards, beet greens, spinach,	3 to 6	4 to 7
Yam, in cubes	7 to 9	9 to 11	kale, turnip greens, swiss chard) chopped		
Turnip, chunks	2 to 4	4 to 6	Green beans, whole	2 to 3	3 to 4
Tomatoes, whole	3 to 5	5 to 7	Escarole, chopped	1 to 2	2 to 3
Tomatoes, in quarters	2 to 3	4 to 5	Endive	1 to 2	2 to 3
Sweet potato, whole, small	10 to 12	12 to 14	Eggplant, chunks or slices	2 to 3	3 to 4
Sweet potato, whole, large	12 to 15	15 to 19	Corn, on the cob	3 to 4	4 to 5
Sweet potato, in cubes	7 to 9	9 to 11	Corn, kernels	1 to 2	2 to 3
Sweet pepper, slices or chunks	1 to 3	2 to 4	Collard	4 to 5	5 to 6
Squash, butternut, slices or chunks	8 to 10	10 to 12	Celery, chunks	2 to 3	3 to 4
Squash, acorn, slices or chunks	6 to 7	8 to 9	Cauliflower flowerets	2 to 3	3 to 4
Spinach	1 to 2	3 to 4	Carrots, whole or chunked	2 to 3	3 to 4
Rutabaga, slices	3 to 5	4 to 6	Carrots, sliced or shredded	1 to 2	2 to 3
Rutabaga, chunks	4 to 6	6 to 8	Cabbage, red, purple or green, wedges	3 to 4	4 to 5
Pumpkin, small slices or chunks	4 to 5	6 to 7	Cabbage, red, purple or green, shredded	2 to 3	3 to 4
Pumpkin, large slices or chunks	8 to 10	10 to 14	Brussel sprouts, whole	3 to 4	4 to 5
Potatoes, whole, large	12 to 15	15 to 19	Broccoli, stalks	3 to 4	4 to 5
Potatoes, whole, baby	10 to 12	12 to 14	Broccoli, flowerets	2 to 3	3 to 4
Potatoes, in cubes	7 to 9	9 to 11	Beets, small roots, whole	11 to 13	13 to 15
Peas, in the pod	1 to 2	2 to 3	Beets, large roots, whole	20 to 25	25 to 30
Peas, green	1 to 2	2 to 3	Beans, green/yellow or wax,	1 to 2	2 to 3
Parsnips, sliced	1 to 2	2 to 3	whole, trim ends and strings		
Parsnips, chunks	2 to 4	4 to 6	Asparagus, whole or cut	1 to 2	2 to 3
Onions, sliced	2 to 3	3 to 4	Artichoke, whole, trimmed without leaves	9 to 11	11 to 13
Okra	2 to 3	3 to 4	Artichoke, hearts	4 to 5	5 to 6

Rice and Grains

Rice & Grain	Water Quantity (Grain: Water ratios)	Cooking Time (in Minutes)	Rice & Grain	Water Quantity (Grain: Water ratios)	Cooking Time (in Minutes)
Wheat berries	1:3	25 to 30	Oats, steel-cut	1:1	10
Spelt berries	1:3	15 to 20	Oats, quick cooking	1:1	6
Sorghum	1:3	20 to 25	Millet	1:1	10 to 12
Rice, wild	1:3	25 to 30	Kamut, whole	1:3	10 to 12
Rice, white	1:1.5	8	Couscous	1:2	5 to 8
Rice, Jasmine	1:1	4 to 10	Corn, dried, half	1:3	25 to 30
Rice, Brown	1:1.3	22 to 28	Congee, thin	1:6 ~ 1:7	15 to 20
Rice, Basmati	1:1.5	4 to 8	Congee, thick	1:4 ~ 1:5	15 to 20
Quinoa, quick cooking	1:2	8	Barley, pot	1:3 ~ 1:4	25 to 30
Porridge, thin	1:6 ~ 1:7	15 to 20	Barley, pearl	1:4	25 to 30

Appendix 3: The Dirty Dozen and Clean Fifteen

The Dirty Dozen and Clean Fifteen

The Environmental Working Group (EWG) is a nonprofit, nonpartisan organization dedicated to protecting human health and the environment Its mission is to empower people to live healthier lives in a healthier environment. This organization publishes an annual list of the twelve kinds of produce, in sequence, that have the highest amount of pesticide residue-the Dirty Dozen-as well as a list of the fifteen kinds ofproduce that have the least amount of pesticide residue-the Clean Fifteen.

THE DIRTY DOZEN	THE CLEAN FIFTEEN
• The 2016 Dirty Dozen includes the following produce. These are considered among the year's most important produce to buy organic:	• The least critical to buy organically are the Clean Fifteen list. The following are on the 2016 list:

THE DIRTY DOZEN

Strawberries	Spinach
Apples	Tomatoes
Nectarines	Bell peppers
Peaches	Cherry tomatoes
Celery	Cucumbers
Grapes	Kale/collard greens
Cherries	Hot peppers

• *The Dirty Dozen list contains two additional itemskale/collard greens and hot peppers-because they tend to contain trace levels of highly hazardous pesticides.*

THE CLEAN FIFTEEN

Avocados	Papayas
Corn	Kiw
Pineapples	Eggplant
Cabbage	Honeydew
Sweet peas	Grapefruit
Onions	Cantaloupe
Asparagus	Cauliflower
Mangos	

• *Some of the sweet corn sold in the United States are made from genetically engineered (GE) seedstock. Buy organic varieties of these crops to avoid GE produce.*

Made in United States
Troutdale, OR
04/17/2024

19237273R00062